GERALD & GERALDINE
(A Testimony Of Age)

GERALD
AND GERALDINE
(A Testimony Of Age)

By
Geraldine (and Gerald)

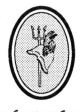

HERMES
2 Tavistock Chambers, Bloomsbury Way, London WC1A 2SE

First Published 1994

ISBN 1 86032 015 5

Typesetting by Jim Barry

Cover illustration by Nikola Hinton

Made and printed in Great Britain by Booksprint, Bristol, England

Introduction

Since the age of eight years, I have never lost sight of my determination to write a book. Yet not until this year, 1993, in my mid-eighties, am I at last making a bold start. It was during the First World War when I announced my intention to a group of female relatives including, probably, my mother, and it was then I first heard of "Uncle" Gerald, himself a well-known author. The information excited me enormously, and from that moment the jig-saw puzzle of our joint lives began to take shape, although until quite recently it showed little sign of ever nearing completion.

As we were never able to meet except in my infancy (blotted from memory) any development seemed doomed to be frustrated.

The one thing I wish to stress now is that I have spared no pains to base the whole story on fact, with the exception of our own names and place-names being changed (apart from London, Manchester, Guildford and Thirlmere).

Gerald Cumberland was his pen-name, so I have chosen Geraldine to make the bond seem closer, as in due course I came to realise our relationship was (and still is) closer than I had been led to believe. The story makes this clear at the outset, and I speak throughout directly to my readers, copiously supplemented by extracts from Gerald's own works.

PART ONE

Chapter One

EARLIEST YEARS

I was born in Manchester during the first decade of the 20th century, and consider myself lucky to still be in reasonably good health during the last decade. My mother's husband, Bill, was not the type of man to be successful as husband or father, being an alcoholic. When he had any money he would go on a spree, and mother would never know when he would return. He often left her in a state of penury. He was supposed to leave home each morning to seek orders for the family's chemical business. However, that did not fit in with his lifestyle; in fact he hated it, frequently refusing to get up. Naturally mother would lose her temper, as she was in desperate circumstances. He never raged back, but would just clear off. She once told me when I was a teenager, that all the time she was pregnant, she was so distraught that she couldn't believe I would be born sane. I understood that her troubles were all due to my 'dad's' impecunious habits, and certainly they were ample cause for her misery. It must have been a great temporary relief that I arrived in good physical condition (certainly not underweight), with apparently no striking resemblance to my real father, obviously no other than Gerald, Bill's younger brother. This is by no means a mystery tale, nor yet an autobiography, as from now on, it will concern little more than the shadowy though definite relationship, occupying most of this century, in spite of Gerald's death only a quarter of the way through. But I must keep my promise and refrain from the temptation to wander into a byway of mystery. I mentioned in the introduction, "Gerald Cumberland was his pen name," so you will readily understand that it was mainly through his writings that he cast such a lasting spell over me. Whether my mother was sure of my parentage I cannot tell. She managed to struggle along for two years after my birth, but the event made no difference to Bill, so that finally she felt obliged to return to her nursing profession, as her maiden sister offered to take charge of me. During those two years no doubt, Gerald would visit us from time to time. He was then a poor clerk in a waterproof works in Salford, apparently unattached, so I am sure he would give whatever help he could. Unfortunately I have no recollection of him whatever.

My mother being very timid and apprehensive, would probably discourage him from making any fuss of me, but I have since acquired unmistakable evidence of his devotion, which persisted throughout the years.

I cannot pause to be more explicit now, as I am trying to adhere to some chronological order. Everything will be revealed in due course. All I remember of those formative years was a gramophone, complete with horn, which I believe belonged to a neighbour. Neither Bill nor mother showed any great interest in music, but as soon as I could talk I was singing in perfect tune from all accounts.

Mother taught me the 'pop' songs of the period, including 'All the Nice Girls Love the Sailors' and 'Pretty Little Girl from Nowhere.' At that time Gerald fancied himself as a musical critic, and about the time when I was taken from Manchester to live for the rest of my childhood in the Lake District, he entered journalism with 'The Manchester Courier,' and became Gerald Cumberland. The choice of surname was significant. After our all too brief contact, the wrench for him must have been a tragic blow, with no further prospect of our ever meeting. I have no reason to suppose that he ever felt any deep attachment to my mother. Probably on the day of conception, having a hunch that Bill was absent, he would call out of sympathy, and be prepared to help if necessary. Mother may even have been driven to have requested a small loan. She would be too proud to turn to her own family, who had to struggle to make ends meet, but the time was now imminent when she could no longer be independent. Whatever speculation I may make, the one certain fact that could not be ignored, was that from that vital day she was confronted with a new daunting problem.

At this point in my narrative I realise that I have already broken my rule of chronology, and made an unforgivable leap backwards of three years. I will try to make amends, and perhaps after all, that little diversion was inevitable under the circumstances. Let us return to the choice of the name Cumberland. Throughout Gerald's earthly life I had given it scarcely a thought, but when the jig-saw puzzle began to take shape in the distant future, the reason suddenly became apparent. Cumberland was then the name of the main county of the Lake District, which had robbed Gerald of his little daughter. My mother's family home address was more to the south, but he was never likely to know that. She could not be sure that he would never seek me out, which must be prevented, as the 'uncle' theory might easily be detected as false by her discerning sisters.

She never divorced Bill, and when later he went to work in a northern shipyard, she occasionally visited him when on holiday, and I recall at least once when she took me with her. Also my new home was accessible for him, and he was always made welcome by my aunts and uncles. They liked him, as he was free and easy, and loved a joke.

In spite of his faults, he seemed popular with the adults, who pitied rather than criticised him. For my part, I too felt sorry for him, but I regarded him as an outsider, and never experienced any trace of affection, which seemed just as lacking on his part, although he had no reason to doubt he was my father any more than I had. On two occasions I remember he bought me a small doll. I will end this chapter with my double-edged story about Lake Thirlmere - strange and disturbing - which will always haunt me. Again I must make a leap in time, and I have to admit some obscurity with regard to my understanding of the two events which insist on being linked. I will begin, believe it or not, by relating the earlier incident first!

This is described in Gerald's wonderful novel 'A Lover at Forty.' The title refers to Basil Trent, a character based to some extent on the author, who was himself about that age at the time of writing. I will now introduce my first extract from one of his works, in which Trent describes haltingly to his fiancee, the lake that had such a staggering effect on me about six years later.

"I've seen it only once. It lies by the side of Helvellyn; the mountain is rooted in its waters. I walked by its side some - eight - years ago. It was a stormy evening, black with clouds, and the lake was leaden, mysterious and cold. It had nothing to say. I remember it so well, Avril. It was very near and yet, somehow, it seemed a long, long way off. It had nothing whatever to say to me."

It was perfectly plain to me that Gerald could not have produced such a chilling impression without having actually encountered the scene. The question that strikes me is - why was it introduced, as it had no bearing on the story, and seemed on the surface, quite irrelevant? Yet the girl Avril bore a slight subtle resemblance to the dark lake. After pondering over it for some time, I realised that it was intended specially for me. I juggled with dates, and concluded that Gerald's visit had occurred shortly after my removal to the Lake District in March 1911. He had made his way to Thirlmere, right in the heart of

Cumberland, and obviously unaccompanied. He could not hope to find me there, but I feel convinced that he had yearned for some kind of spiritual contact, which would leave a warm glow in his sad heart. Alas, it had nothing to say - nothing whatever to say to him. The lake was leaden, mysterious, cold - in fact remote and cut off from all touch of humanity.

On my first visit a few years later, not knowing of Gerald's contact, I could not differ from his verdict, yet those very characteristics appealed to me tremendously. I had been nursed in the lush greenery farther south, and appreciated its gentle harmonious beauty; but the almost sudden stark contrast of Thirlmere's solitary crags excited and thrilled me. Instead of human habitations there were caves to shelter the wild creatures; and the untamed Spirit of Nature was present everywhere. Poor Gerald! It was not the Spirit of Nature that he had sought, but I do believe he left behind a trace of his own untrammelled spirit, which still haunted the region on my venture there; it greeted me with the inspiration I needed, but no warmth, an abundance of which had already filled my life to the point of suffocation.

13

Chapter Two

A FEW PERSONAL REMINISCENCES

After Gerald's disappointingly abortive visit to the unwelcoming Cumberland lake of Thirlmere, I like to think of him returning to Manchester, probably still in 1911, wisely determined to make the best of his life, and accept the inevitable. Thirlmere had snubbed him, and so far as I know, he never returned to Cumberland, though retaining the name. But for me, I was anchored at Beckside throughout childhood, so our paths never crossed. I would be about seventeen when he died, but news of the event did not reach me at the time. As for Bill, he died while I was taking my final examinations at College. I shed some compassionate tears, but we had not been in contact for many years, so it made no difference to my life. As far as I can make out, Gerald met and married the German girl Esther, in 1912 or 1913, in Manchester before being lured to London's Fleet Street.

Years later Gerald (himself no moralist) wrote: "One loves and pities a poor fellow whose temperament has made him a wastrel." Surely he must have been thinking of brother Bill and their two lives so divergent, yet which crossed so strangely.

I have already given up all pretence of adhering to that chronological idea, simply because Gerald's books make it impossible without constant irritating cross references. He had written two books that he termed 'Reminiscences,' with 'Lover at Forty' sandwiched uncomfortably between them. The Reminiscences were by no means presented in an orderly or

15

disciplined fashion; for instance, as a preface to the second one he notes:

"Some of the following pages have appeared during the last four years in 'The Century Magazine,' 'Punch,' 'The Saturday Review,' 'The Sunday Chronicle,' 'The Humorist' and 'Musical Opinion,' but much of the greater part of the volume is now printed for the first time." It was dated May 1923, three years before his death. Yet, on the last page he recalls: "... in 1912, I was about to leave Manchester for London."

Finding such definite dates which were important to me, was like looking for the proverbial needle in the haystack. Therefore I give up with a sigh of relief. I will begin at the beginning of his first book regardless, and report what I fancy as I progress through the text once more.

So good-bye to chronology, and this short chapter. The next one is likely to consist almost solely of extracts from Gerald's first meeting with Bernard Shaw. It was also my first literary 'meeting' with Gerald, which won my joyous and lasting affection. I was then in my mid thirties when a friend came across a copy of the book which proved such a treasure.

Chapter Three

SHAW FEVER

The first Book of Reminiscences was published in 1919. I will copy the Preface, written in Winchester in 1918.

"Very many of the following pages were written in the trenches and dug-outs of Greece and Serbia. I added a chapter or two in Port Said, Alexandria and Marseilles. That is to say, I wrote far away from books and without reference to documents, and I wrote to refresh a mind dulled by the conditions of Active Service in the Near East. A few chapters were written in London and a few in Winchester.

Here and there may be found factual inaccuracies, though if these exist I am not aware of them. But the spirit of the book is as near the truth as I can bring it."

I feel humbled and ashamed at the thought of the various criticisms with which I confronted him in my draft copy of this work, but now, making one of my predictable leaps into the future, we understand each other perfectly, and on my part all is admiration and affection, actually increased by any peccadilloes that have crept in unbidden. After all, they were usually accompanied by a wonderful teasing humour which wins every little tussle, and is just as much part of him as the 'spirit' so often referred to, and of necessity mentioned in that last sentence of the Preface. And now to the beginning of the first chapter of his book, entitled 'George Bernard Shaw.'

There is so little I feel justified in cutting, but I am privileged to be the means of resurrecting much that has lain dormant undeservedly for so long.

"It was when I was a very young man that I caught and succumbed to my first attack of Shaw-fever. I do not remember how I caught it; something in the Manchester air, no doubt, was responsible for my malady, for a handful of 'intellectual' Manchester people had most daringly produced a complete Shaw play. I had read it, and it was with delight that I saw the Manchester Guardian saying about 'You Never Can Tell' just the very things I had myself already thought. I found that in my suburban circle of friends I was regarded as harbouring 'advanced ideas.'

Shaw, I was told, was 'dangerous'. This bucked me up enormously, and I thereupon wrote a long essay on Ibsen's 'A Doll's House' and, desiring further to astonish and bewilder my friends, I got into communication with Bernard Shaw with a view to having the essay published in pamphlet form.

When it was known in Manchester suburbia that Shaw had written to me, a boy still at school, my friends could not decide whether I was cleverer than they had hitherto supposed, or Mr. Bernard Shaw more foolish than seemed possible. I have never completely recovered from that first attack of Shaw-fever; like ague, it sleeps in my bones and, from time to time, makes its presence known by little convulsions that are disturbing enough while they last, but which generally die pretty quickly.

It was in the middle of 1901 that I wrote to Mr. Shaw about the particular brand of socialism from which at that time I was suffering. It must have been a very raw and crude brand, and my letter must have amused him considerably. Certainly his reply was most diverting. Here it is:

'By all means give every penny you can spare to those who are most in need of monetary help. If you will be kind enough to send it to the Treasurer of the Fabian Society, you may depend upon its being wanted and well used. If you prefer relieving needy persons, I can give you the names and addresses of several fathers of families who can be depended on to absorb all your superfluous resources, however vast they may be. By making yourself poor for their sakes you will have the satisfaction of adding one more poor family to the existing mass of poverty, and contributing your utmost to the ransom which perpetuates the existing social system. You will go through life consoled by an inexhaustible sense of moral superiority to bishops and other inconsistent Christians. And you will never be at a loss for friends. Where the carcass is, there will the eagles be gathered.

A world of beggars and almsgivers - beautiful Christian ideal. You are not a prig - only a damned fool. A month's experience will cure you.'

I know not in what terms of pained surprise and hurt vanity I replied, but a few days later I received the following short note: 'Yes, you are an ass; and nothing will help you until you get over that. I strongly recommend you to become a stockbroker. You believe that doing good means giving money; and you fancy yourself in the character of Lord Bountiful with a touch of St. Francis. Yes, a hopeless ass. No matter; embrace your destiny and become a philanthropist. It is not a bad life for people who are built that way.'

That I think most effectively closed the correspondence."

But not for long - it was not the end of their relationship. Gerald had become involved with the publishers Greening and Co., over their 'Eminent Writers of To-day' series. He had completed a commissioned book on Hall Caine, and conceived the idea of writing one about Shaw. He communicated with him, informing him of his intention, and asking if he would provide him with biographical details. He agreed and at the end of 1901 (Gerald then about 21) wrote from his Guildford home, saying, "If you will let me know when you are coming to London, I will make an appointment with pleasure and give you what help I can." I leave it to Gerald to continue the narrative.

"A few weeks later I went to Guildford, but with a guilty secret hidden in my breast. My publishers did not care about issuing a complete book devoted to Shaw and all his works. I gathered, much to my amazement that they did not think him of sufficient importance. The astounding idea was suggested that half my book should be concerned with Bernard Shaw and the other half with George Moore. At the time of my Guildford visit, I had not imparted this information to Shaw. I did not anticipate that he would like the suggestion, and I thought it wiser to disclose it to him by word of mouth rather than by letter.

I came upon Mr. Shaw taking photographs in his little front garden. It was a winter's day and an inch of snow lay upon the ground; yet he wore no overcoat. He insisted upon taking my photograph. He took me sitting. He took me standing. And when he had grown tired of playing with his new toy, he suggested that we should go into the house. There a hideous surprise awaited me. Lying upon the sofa of the study was an open copy of the current week's 'Candid Friend,' a most brilliant and ruthless paper edited by Frank Harris.

'There is something there,' said Shaw, nodding in the direction of the sofa, 'that should interest you.' I sat down, took up the paper and looked at the open pages.

To my horror I saw a most brutal, murderously clever full-page caricature of Hall Caine on one side, and on the other a long and most hostile review of my stupid little book on the famous novelist... Shaw, tall and erect, stood looking at me a little malignantly, and, on the instant, I was on my guard.

I read the review and examined the caricature. The article was amazingly good, but, as I read it, I did so wish it had been written about a book by somebody else. Frank Harris himself, I think, had written the article, and Frank Richardson had drawn the caricature. I looked up at Shaw and smiled. 'Awfully good, don't you think?' I said. He nodded, and by his manner seemed to express approval of the way in which I had come through the ordeal.

He showed me some photographs he had taken - not very good photographs. One, taken by his wife, showed him with his arm round a female scarecrow; leaning slightly forward, he was leering at it with narrowed eyes."

I suppose I should have avoided these trivialities, but to me they were irresistible nevertheless. Gerald continues:

"During lunch Shaw devoured a large number of vegetarian dishes and drank water, while Mrs. Shaw and I ate meat and drank wine. It was, I think, the mellowing influence of a basin of raisins that loosed his tongue and set him talking without cessation. He spoke of Karl Marx...., of Sidney Webb and the Fabian Society, of Morocco and Ancoats, of Shorthand and Wagner, of The Manchester Guardian and H.G. Wells. I rather gathered that he had 'got over' Karl Marx years ago, and inferred that he considered the work of this writer indispensable for young cubs to sharpen their teeth upon, but that he was by no means the last word in socialism. I think he thought that Bernard Shaw was the last word."

I will cut out his remarks about Annie Besant and Janet Achurch, which I found less entertaining.

"Of Sidney Webb I remember nothing that he said, nor have any of the loving words he spoke of the Fabian Society remained in my memory. He spoke of it a great deal, back at lunch and during our subsequent walk, but somehow or other it has always seemed to me a bloodless and dull sort of institution, and while he talked about it my thoughts wandered, and I mused rather sadly over the psychology of this man whose moral earnestness was so much greater than my own."

I will skip over the remains of the lunch and concentrate on the much more diverting afternoon programme. I cannot resist quoting in detail Gerald at his best.

"Never shall I forget that terrible walk. I believed then, as I believe now, that Shaw was deliberately pitting his powers of endurance against my own - the powers of endurance of a middle-aged vegetarian against those of a young meat-eater. He walked with a long, easy stride, swinging his arms, breathing deeply through his wide nostrils. His pace, which never for a moment did he attempt to accommodate to mine, was at least five miles an hour.

He forgot, or he did not choose to remember, that I had that morning travelled by the slow midnight train from Manchester, that I had crossed London, that I had reached Guildford by a weary Sunday train from Waterloo, and that I had just eaten an enormous lunch. I panted and struggled half a pace behind him. I became stupendously hot. I made unexpected and unathletic sounds, like a man who is being smothered. Blissfully unconscious of all this was Shaw.... I wonder?... No; blissfully conscious of all this was Shaw.

He talked steadily the whole time, but I was suffering from an inhibition of all my mental faculties. Yet, at the back of my mind, I kept saying to myself: 'You know, you have not yet told him that he is to share your book with George Moore.' And each time I told myself that, I shuddered somewhat. It was not until we had neared G. F. Watts' house that Shaw moderated his pace a little. 'That' said he, in a curiously low voice - the kind of voice one uses in churches - 'that is where G.F. Watts lives.' And he pointed to some high chimneys that overtopped a belt of trees, and stopped and gazed. But I was in no mood of reverence and, though I have frequently struggled to induce a feeling of rapture when gazing upon the large canvases of Watts, I have never been able to do so. So I pulled out my handkerchief and wiped my perspiring forehead.

'Hot?' asked Shaw grimly.

'Of course I'm hot. Aren't you?'

'Warm. Just nicely warm.'

Presently we came to a tall tower of terra-cotta bricks which, Shaw told me, had been erected by the villagers under the direction and at the instigation of Watts himself. We stopped in front of this and, as it was one of the 'sights' of the district, I felt that I was expected to say something wise or, at all events, something complimentary about it. I could say neither.

'Which do people imagine it to be - useful or ornamental?' I asked.

'I wonder,' said he.

'For it is neither,' I ventured.

But his thoughts were 'otherwhere,' for he began a long technical exposition on the art of making bricks and tiles. His talk became art-and-crafty. I was carried back to my childhood days, my kindergarten days. I heard the name of William Morris, and I sighed most profoundly. Shaw won that walk by a neck. Having reached his home, he put me in a kind of conservatory, gave me a blanket and a deck chair and told me to go to sleep. But already I was asleep...

Later, after tea, when Mrs. Shaw had left the room, I broached the subject of my book. 'Publishers are curious people', I remarked. He sat silent. 'My own publishers in particular. They are now fighting shy of a book solely about you.' I paused and glanced at him. But he was gazing at me with eyes of a mild malice, and he was very silent.

'Yes' I continued, 'to put it bluntly, they think that a book solely about you would not be a success. So they propose the first half of the book should be concerned with you, and the second half with George Moore.'

'And the title?' he asked gently.

'Why? What do you mean?'

'Well, don't you think 'The Two Mad Irishmen' would go rather well?'

I floundered. If he was going to be witty or sarcastic or anything horrid of that kind, I should be nowhere at all. To cover my confusion - and, as it chanced, to make that confusion worse - I began to talk very rapidly." (But I will pass over the rest of that painful-for-Gerald flop). Shaw not surprisingly had the last word. 'I shall wash my hands of the whole business.' Gerald adds later: "He walked with me down to the station. He droned on about Sidney Webb and the Fabian Society... So many people have talked to me of Sidney Webb. I wonder why.

I have heard him speak; he knows about figures and dates and money and wages, and so on... But, of human nature he knows nothing; he knows less than a child, for a child has at least intuition. Figures don't go very far, do they? Of course, by manipulation, you can make them go all the way....

But, as I was saying, Shaw talked about Fabianism and Webbism all the way to the station. He was good enough to wait till the train started, and the last I saw of him as I leaned through the window was a long, lean figure standing under a lamp."

I can't help concluding that, in spite of some awkward moments caused by Shaw deliberately, he had a little fond feeling for Gerald, partly, but not entirely because a considerable element of amusement was never far from the surface. I have been unable to do much pruning to Gerald's first chapter of his Reminiscences, for the simple reason that I could identify myself in all the situations - his early type of socialism, his ultra boredom with detailed conversations about money matters, and his lack of interest in arty-crafty products. However the mention of William Morris should not have caused such a profound sigh. I can share his lack of enthusiasm for Morris's Artistic designs, but I trust, Gerald that one obvious gap in your early education has been rectified, namely the fact that Morris was first and foremost a Socialist of the highest grade, in spite of the wealth and privileges that he inherited.

Why am I suddenly speaking directly to Gerald who left this world about three generations ago? One thing is certain - he is very much alive over the Border, wiser and still learning, evidence of which I will reveal by degrees, but the opportune moment has not yet appeared.

Chapter Four

CONFUSION & INTOXICATION

In spite of professing early in the last chapter some contrition over certain criticisms of Gerald that I had made from time to time in my draft copy, I feel obliged after all to repeat the most obvious of them, if only in order to present a more balanced image to my readers. After all he admits to being guilty of 'malice,' but I assure him that I harbour no trace whatever of malice in any of my remarks or feelings towards him. The following quote, straight from the horse's mouth, gives an example of a totally acceptable criticism of character defects being immediately followed by unacceptable comments on physical defects.

"Nothing is more distressing and repellent to me than affectation, and the affectation of most members of the Theosophical Society whom I met was really appalling. The people were also grotesque. The pale men had dyspepsia and bald heads and the women wore djibbahs and a look of condescending benevolence. One of these bald-pated freaks is well known to me. He delivers lectures. He has written books. He passes judgement. He annotates. He writes an occasional review. Funny little freak! Great little freak, who knows so much and understands so little."

I agree wholeheartedly about being repelled by affectation, but Gerald doesn't make it clear whether affectation causes loss of hair, or whether baldness drives men to become affected (a sort of compensatory cover-up?). Gerald sinks to his lowest ebb over the 'great little freak.' Why is the poor nameless fellow described as funny? After all, those five pithy, sentences could well refer to himself just substituting 'He' for 'I.' It seems obvious that the little freak has won his epithet of 'freak' mainly through being 'little' in stature. I wonder why he remains nameless, unlike Norman Angell "small but magisterial... a queer little chap?" Gerald admits he felt 'vaguely discomfited' when Angell (wrongly as it happened) prophesied that the war would soon be over. Clearly, those who hated the war and were up to the eyes in the struggle for peace, were also regarded by many as freaks, but of a new-fangled type, therefore as 'dangerous' as Bernard Shaw.

Gerald you must forgive me. Now, in the Beyond, most of the dark clouds of ignorance will have vanished, leaving a clear path forward to the light of true knowledge.

I keep forgetting you were my father, as I believe such relationships cease to exist when we cast aside our earthly coils. After all, I am writing as a very old woman, who ought to have acquired a considerable stock of wisdom from her vast experience of life. What use is that wisdom if it fails to include detailed memories of what it really was like to be young? And you, poor Gerald, crammed so much into your short life, including the war years; was it surprising that you failed to see through the fog and beyond? Your constant study of the individuals who made up most of your general education, taught you many valuable lessons, probably more than the study of books, but none of us understood all the most vital secrets of our World as it then appeared, let alone the Universe. We must all learn to seek and find the Truth, which is full of excitement but often uncomfortable and almost terrifying.

Even I, at my advanced age have just, through your guidance, learned the most reassuring lesson of all - the fact of an after life of great opportunities, unhampered by a finite body ever subjected to accident, disease, pain and anguish. Yet, this life is a preparation, and my faith (not a religious one) is that we should make the best of it by working for a fair share of Mother Earth's Bounty and Beauty for all her inhabitants.

I have a great urge to end this chapter by burying the bogey of 'Frank Harris.' I will quote a few odd remarks of Gerald's before venturing my own brief reactions.

"From the very first moment he intoxicated me" (at Manchester's Midland Hotel after Harris had endured 'a rotten journey from London and felt unutterably bored.') All Gerald recalled of his conversation before the lecture was that Harris, with some venom, called Browning 'a not unprosperous gentleman.'

An ominous irrelevant warning. Gerald writes of the local dramatic society audience.

"To this assembly of earnest, pale men and spectacled women .... From the very first daring theories, anathematising all forms of respectability .... condemning, en bloc, the whole human race, and particularly that portion of it seated before him. Ladies rustled; men stirred uneasily. Then, having delivered himself of a passage of hot eloquence, he paused. A clock ticked. He looked defiantly at us and still paused..... Thrusting out his chin, he began again.

And this time he attacked the Mancunian literary idol, Professor Herford, a great scholar, but a more than suitable object for Harris's ridicule. Herford is a man who has not lived fully: a semi-invalid, asthmatic, bloodless and spectacled; a man of books and rather dusty books; in effect a professor.

He had recently reviewed Harris's book, 'The Man Shakespeare', in the Manchester Guardian, and called it 'a disgrace to British scholarship'. Why this should have annoyed the author I cannot tell, but Harris is at times a little unreasonable. Indeed 'annoyance' but feebly describes the feeling that spent itself in scalding invective and the most terrible irony. Each sentence he spoke appeared to be the last word in bitterness; but each succeeding sentence leaped above and beyond its predecessor, until at length the speaker had lashed himself into a state of feeling, to express which, words were useless. He stopped magnificently, and this time the room rang with applause. It is probable that not half a dozen people present believed his attack on Herford was justified; indeed it is probable that not half-a-dozen were qualified to form any opinion of value on the matter. Nevertheless they applauded him with enthusiasm, and they did so because they had been deeply stirred by eloquence that can only be described as superb, and by anger that was lava hot in its sincerity. Briefly, the lecture was an overwhelming success. I was soon to discover that Harris like all the men of genius I have met, is vain."

Gerald continues for another twelve pages, but I have quoted enough to prove that not only was Harris vain (most men have some vanity and it can at times be endearing) but this outburst was the sheer, cruel, unadulterated conceit of a cowardly bully which I could never forgive. He believed he was the Centre of the Universe. Eventually, the God turned out a Midget and the Universe rejected it.

Chapter Five

A FISH OUT OF WATER

I am drawn still closer to Gerald by his enlightened attitude to women, probably first influenced by Bernard Shaw. His schoolboy essay on Ibsen's 'Doll's House' indicated plainly that he had already leaped far in advance of his parental Tory background. To his great credit, he took up the cause of the suffragettes at the time when they were being brutally treated, as he had witnessed at first-hand.

His open hostility to bigotry in religion also touched me to the core. To his surprise he was once asked to be guest at the annual dinner of the Church Diocesan Music Society. The following quote yet again proves our close affinity re. fun and humour.

"I am always ready for adventure, of however hazardous a nature, so I accepted the invitation even after I had been told that a speech was expected from me.
Bishop Welldon plumped himself on a chair next to me, and immediately began to dominate everything and everybody within a radius of twenty yards. He is one of those distressing people who will be jocular. And his jocularity is rather noisy. He laughed a great deal, and rubbed his hands together. And he asked me a question and then asked me another before I had time to answer the first.... I had prepared a fierce and warlike speech, a speech attacking the Society whose food I had just eaten, and whose wine was still warm in my veins. I am, I suppose, quite the worst speaker in the world; so I had memorised

my speech, and so good I thought it, that I had vastly enjoyed doing so. But alas! When the minute drew near for me to deliver it, I found myself in an atmosphere of such conviviality, such kindness, such flattering attention that I could not find it in my heart to deliver the words I had prepared and memorised. Yet an impromptu speech of a different tenor was impossible. I simply hadn't the talent to do it. My name was called and I rose to my feet. My speech was offensive: it was meant to be. I mentioned the name of Wagner and, as I did so, I saw Dr. Walford Davies shudder most violently. Though I attacked the Church for her unimaginative attitude to music, though I stamped on hymns and hymn tunes, though I slammed the microscopic brains of many organists, though I said that nearly all Cathedral music was to me anathema, nobody except Bishop Welldon appeared to care, apart from poor virginal Walford Davies, who, at the name of Wagner, shuddered and put his glass aside.

Davies spoke: earnestly like St. Francis; frenziedly like Savonarola; passionately like Venus... no! no! no!.... passionately like St. Paul. Eschew Wagner!

That's what it all came to... Eschew.... Hate the sin, love the sinner, but most certainly 'eschew' both. His cheeks were very white, his lips pale. He trembled a little. Wagner, it appeared, was one of the devils. Ab-so-lute-ly pernicious. Have you ever noticed how accurately you can estimate a man by his adjectives? Dr. Walford Davies used 'pernicious' eleven times, 'poisonous' twice, 'very-much-to-be-distrusted' once, 'naughty' once ('this naughty man!' was the phrase), 'unlicensed' twice, and 'immoral' 15 times... I must say that I am writing from memory, and that my memory for figures is atrocious; still, these adjectives, collectively represent the impression that the speech of this cultured gentleman had left on my mind.

After dinner one does not ardently desire a speech of that kind. It fell flat. A fat organist from Bolton (or was it Bacup?) winked me a fat wink. The man on my left - a young musical doctor from Cambridge - dug his elbow into my ribs.

And then came Bishop Welldon's speech. He was extraordinarily clever; he said some of the most cutting things imaginable; he was scathing; he hurt me; and he spoke so well; he had presence; he had a manner;...

Most of the diners, remembering that Bishop Welldon was indeed a bishop - though, truly, only so to speak an ex-bishop, and an ex-bishop only of Calcutta, and now possessing only the powers of a dean - most of the diners recollecting that Bishop Welldon was indeed a bishop, looked at me with eyes of faint hostility, or did not look at me at all.

I was very young, said Bishop Welldon. I was enthusiastic, I was inexperienced. I was 'artistic', I was a jumper-at-conclusions.

Later on in the evening, Bishop Welldon, a little group of jolly people and I myself sat and smoked and drank coffee. Dr. Walford Davies did not join us. He shot little pointed darts at me from his eyes, but (as of course you must have anticipated) when he and I parted, he was most studiously polite.

And on my way to my tram, I hummed Davies' 'Hame! Hame! Hame!' to myself, and pondered over the mystery that enables a man to write such a wonderful, soul-searching melody, and yet possess an intellect of quality only .... well, so - so.

'Here a little child I stand Heaving up my either hand.'

Do you know Walford Davies' setting of that Grace? If you do, if, as I do, you adore its Blake-like simplicity, its Ariel freshness, you will not mind his hatred of Wagner. Only, it is rather strange, that we outsiders who love Wagner (and must be rather outsiderish?) should be able to love Walford Davies also, though he can't or won't love us."

Well, I don't go quite all the way with Gerald in being touched by Walford Davies' child's Grace, but I was happy to realise he shared my love of Blake's simplicity, as a contrast to our mutual supreme regard for Wagner.

Amazingly, from page twenty nine in the 'Malice' Reminiscences to page two hundred and twenty five in the same volume, Walford Davies seems to have made a miraculous U-turn! Wagner now appears as a hot favourite! Gerald doesn't remark about this, so perhaps many years had elapsed and dulled his memory of the cultured gentleman. The contradiction had evidently been noted by another earnest fact-finder, but Gerald, I suppose must be forgiven by quoting Walt Whitman's admission:

"Do I contradict myself? Very well, then, I contradict myself."

Chapter Six

INTERVAL

At that point I was laid low for almost three weeks by a chest infection. As it did not respond to the first course of antibiotics, I soon became very despondent as I was quite unable to continue my narrative, or even plan which way it should develop. I blamed myself for not beginning the work earlier, also for including certain details which I now felt would have been better left out. So now I must try to make up for lost time, and decide on some drastic cuttings. I began this chapter at midnight November 30th, with the determination to spend many hours of each December day, in my labour of love, which has now become urgent, as I realise my increasing bodily weakness. The midnight decision may sound overtaxing under my present condition, and already sleep crept on me unawares for a few seconds. However being naturally owlish, the nocturnal venture can easily become a habit after a few days, or rather nights, and as I will still be regarded as a semi-invalid for the rest of my life, I shall be encouraged to sleep whenever nature prompts. Any normal or surprise daytime interruptions will be quite welcome, which are not likely to interfere with general progress. Just then sleep took over completely, until roused by the recurring 'symptoms.' I felt desperate until mid-morning, when I finally tracked down the pill culprits. So now I hope I'm really on the road to recovery.

Chapter Seven

DREAMS & SIGHTINGS (1993)

My recovery has been complicated, and only now late in the day, does my head feel clear enough, and my body rested enough, to continue. As this blissful state is not guaranteed to persist, I have decided to jettison all ideas of chronology and devote all my attention to the present year, the last month of which is already well on its way. After all the second half has proved to be in a gradual, quiet way, crammed with the most important events of my life, the years behind almost unconsciously having pointed guiding fingers from time to time.

I have so far avoided enumerating all the sightings and strange dreams, that this year has brought in its wake. I had hoped to introduce them unhurriedly, as they actually occurred, but my readers must be feeling irritated and impatient, no doubt justifiably so. Therefore I will take the plunge, rather nervously, because I cannot avoid mentioning a vital dream which causes slight embarrassment in the telling.

The dream consisted entirely of a single act of intercourse, culminating in a perfect orgasm. Nothing had led up to it, and nothing followed. It was not excitement I experienced, but a very deep joy of fulfilment. I awoke to realise immediately that no partner had been involved nor could I imagine one who could ever possibly have produced such an effect. It did not haunt me consciously, but I realised about two days later its significance, which had been only gradually coming to light.

About the same time I encountered my ghosts. As I had already recorded this sighting just after it occurred, I will resort to my notes, and do some copying to help conserve my energy.

Several manifestations during the springtime call for investigation and explanation. One beautiful sunny day I made the short walk to the local post office. I passed a small public garden on the way, well-kept, but the one seat had been removed a few weeks earlier, no doubt due to vandalism. On this occasion I noticed two people sitting on a seat near the rear of the garden, well back from the road on each side. The seat appeared to be made just for two.

The figure facing me on the right was a woman with a considerable mass of grey hair, and her companion I took to be a male, but it was only a casual glimpse. 'If they have gone when I come out of the post office', I decided, 'I will sit there for a few minutes and enjoy the sunshine.'

Some of my readers may remember that early spring had been mostly dull, damp and cold, which made us like to take advantage of the odd sunny days, and this was the month of May. When I emerged at least ten minutes later, I glanced across; the two figures were no longer there, and as I approached, I realised that the seat had also vanished! That quite shook me, but not through fear. Each time I thought of the incident during the next two days, I could still recall how the grey-haired lady looked, but the other person had begun to fade, and I wasn't at all sure of the gender. In fact, I could remember no distinguishing features whatever. Each time I thought about it, the figure seemed to diminish in size and significance.

Finally it struck me that the grey-haired person was myself, and as for the little spectral friend, who could that be but Gerald in disguised spirit form. I must here remind you that so far I only knew him from his revealing books, but that was more than sufficient to make me appreciate his tremendous sense of fun and humour, so akin to my own. He was always ready to partake in acts of mischief, and this was undeniably a typical example of his stock of jokes. The jig-saw puzzle was expanding a little. I knew there was more to the event than just a 'youthful' prank. There was obviously a message behind it, and suddenly all was made clear. One thing seemed certain - we were drawing closer together, and it was quite comforting. I began to read Betty Shine's book 'Mind to Mind' just after that, and realised I would never need to be afraid of anything else that Gerald might have in store for me. To recap, the period before 1993 had gradually convinced me that Gerald was definitely my father. The more I read his books (the novel at least as much as the Reminiscences) the more obvious did it become. I was then planning to write my own book, which I felt could be interesting to so many people. Just to be re-united with a 'lost' father through coming across his written works, was surely unusual and intriguing. But I had hesitated, although pretty certain Gerald would approve if conscious of the fact. I must have been just on the threshold of realising our spiritual connection.

But now - the evidence was all around. Suddenly the erotic dream unfolded its message. Here was no joke, but the all-important serious Gerald just letting me know in the most beautiful way imaginable, that I had been the issue of such perfect union. The unlikely ghost scene following so soon afterwards was probably necessary to link it all. Gerald was also making it doubly clear that he understood all my problems and was assuring me that I could go ahead with my 'link' book, relying on his constant encouragement and help.

That was final proof enough for me. He was still a living and loving being, untrammelled by earthly hindrances, and there would be a place for me in the future, among kindred spirits. But there is still a long way to go. Now that I am back in action, I must guard my bodily health tenaciously, in order to reach some kind of conclusion to this unpredictable testimony.

Gerald and I could never disrupt our unique relationship now, and the temporary dual world barrier could cause only minor disagreements. Yet I found myself still foolishly lamenting that Gerald had failed to realise the inherent evil of war in the abstract, and his acceptance of the horrific First World War that had played havoc with two years of his short life, and no doubt helped to bring about his premature death.

By this time I was fully conscious of the fact that he was monitoring my main thoughts, whether or not written down for possible publication. Naturally enough he would not take kindly to my ill-starred criticisms, and he reckoned I must be given a little salutary punishment in the shape of a mildly unpleasant dream. In it I saw a strange caterpillar-like creature 'running' about on my carpet, to be joined by another and yet another. They were too long to be caterpillars, and moved far too quickly, in fact 'running' as fast as mice; yet only on countless tiny feet. The creatures moved in different directions, almost as though playing a game. They were jet black and covered with short hairy spikes, like nothing I had ever seen or imagined. I didn't exactly welcome them, but when I realised three was to be the limit, I accepted them as long as they ignored me.

They seemed to believe that they had been placed there for my entertainment. I watched in amazement, but probably only for a few seconds before I awoke. It dawned on me very soon that the little show had been another of Gerald's tricks, brought about to show some half-hearted displeasure, or a nudge to mind my step! I ceased to regard him as a father figure (if I had ever done so) and reminded myself that he had been little over forty when the 'Friendship' Reminiscences were published, and they included events he recalled when much younger. If he were then mistaken in some of the characters he revered, don't we all tend to go through that phase before our years of 'wisdom' supplant it?

Before the dream just mentioned, I should have described a strange 'sighting' which I am sure had considerable significance. One morning when I was wide awake and just finished breakfast, a bright white light suddenly flashed past close to my window, on the right side only. At precisely the same moment, I felt a sudden sharp, but painless prick in the joint of the first finger of my left hand. The word 'light' is misleading, for it appeared as a frosted object, rapidly changing into the shape more of a fine silky cloth, billowing like the sail of a small boat. I think it had been raining, but the sun was breaking through the fresh white clouds. Instinctively I felt Gerald was happy, and wanting to share his natural joy with me. Then, after the 'black creatures' dream, when under the magical influence of Betty Shine, I felt once more in accord with Gerald, accepting the inevitable differences. In this calm mood of complete reconciliation, another strange 'visitation' occurred. Again I was facing the same window, wide awake, when two fair-sized identical elliptical objects appeared in the sky, just above my tall unpruned privet hedge. They most certainly were not clouds, as they were moving very swiftly, one closely following the other, with just a small space separating them. The colour I can only describe as light brown, which I at once felt was significant. It was neutral, and showed me that Gerald was appreciating my efforts to minimise our minor conflicts. Later I realised the symbolism. Gerald and I from that moment onwards would aim towards the same goal, making light of our differences, and with our minds in harmony.

I experienced several other daylight window flashes from time to time from my kitchen, cut off from all sight and sound of traffic. Incidentally, all the movements I have described were from left to right. In this case the silvery flashes took the form of cutting blades, parallel yet slanting, fairly close, yet one slightly ahead of the other. A few days later two more ordinary

41

lights skimmed past, more like sheet lightning, again very close but not touching. I knew this to be a good omen - just a friendly gesture to prove that Gerald was still around, and all was well.

These friendly demonstrations not only always moved in the same direction, but never appeared singly. The first window sighting had shown two parts merging without a break, yet quite different in shape and texture. The others showed separate entities, yet paradoxically inseparable. The symbolism was quite unmistakable. More recently when I was poring over a small pile of books late at night, I was distracted by some pretty little dancing circles, pale pink, mauve and blue. This time there were more than two, floating gracefully round and round, with no serious message, but pleasantly diverting.

Some people no doubt would believe that my strange sightings are conjured up in my own mind through the power of suggestion, and that I dwell so much on each one that I expect more to follow.

That is definitely untrue, because each one occurred quite independently of the others; each had a different message and meaning, though related. Also, they all took place when my mind was fully occupied with other matters.

One thing I must stress emphatically is the fact that never were my dreams or sightings the result of drug taking on my part. In fact I cannot impress too strongly on all young boys and girls on the threshold of life, to steadfastly refuse even to experiment with drugs. I myself, when fairly young experienced only two occasions when I had been thus affected. The first time was when on a cruise shortly before the outbreak of the war in 1939. I was given a drink which, in a foolish unguarded moment I accepted, with what could easily have resulted in dire consequences. Only by the vigilance of my older and wiser companion on the voyage, did I escape from what could have been a disaster to wreck my life. For probably only a few seconds, I felt in a world of blissful sensation, before being abruptly brought round to my senses.

The second experience was at the dentist's, while under an anaesthetic for the removal of an old infected crowned tooth. I remembered no detail of what must have carried me over the border. Not until the moment of recovering consciousness, was I aware that I had indeed been transfigured. I found myself exclaiming bitterly "Oh, what a mean trick to play on me, to drag me back into this world." Whether the words were actually spoken with my human voice, or just burst unbidden from my spiritual being, I am not sure. It seemed as though I was half way through the protest before I recognised my actual situation.

It was many years later before I read about seriously ill people who claimed to have entered the spirit world for a few moments before being restored to earthly life. Many were able to describe a place of supreme beauty, of glorious colours and an atmosphere of wonderful peace. For myself, I remembered no details, but I believe I was close to death, as the drug had to be extra strong to keep me effectively free from pain.

The dental surgeon and nurse were obviously very concerned at the length of time it took for me to come round. I was so ill that they had to keep me in the surgery for what seemed a long time, before I felt fit to leave. I caught a bus close by for the short ride home, but nearly fainted on entry, and had to ask for a seat in the hot and crowded vehicle. It was straight to bed on arrival home, and at least another day before I returned to normal. That incident occurred about 1943.

Although I had experienced some vague but wonderful out-of-this-world sensations, never for a moment had I any craving to repeat such visions.

I always realised that addiction to drugs meant great damage to both mind and body. I also felt a very strong opposition to achieving happiness by artificial means. I sincerely pity all the poor souls whose ordinary lives provide no lasting satisfaction or happiness, so that they become easy prey to the furtive and evil influence of even light drugs like cannabis. I have seen the effects on others at close quarters, and those who manage to escape from its clutches in time, are lucky indeed.

May all the evil people who make fortunes out of trafficking in drugs, get their deserts in the spirit world. They will not burn in hell fire, as so graphically depicted by certain religions (simply for not conforming to rigid rules), but they will not enjoy life in a paradise reserved for their victims. They will learn the hard way.

On that point I will break off, with one of my dreams still untold. As I regard it as of particular importance, the next chapter will be devoted entirely to the strange story and its significance.

Chapter Eight

THE VITAL VISION

In my dream I found myself just about to leave a huge supermarket. Anything that had happened in the immediate past had been completely blotted from my memory. I sensed a strange environment, and realised that this location could have no place in Britain. The most likely alternative I decided would be Russia, without any obvious evidence. The only real action occurred quite rapidly, but was packed with meaning, which baffled me at the time. I found myself on an escalator leading to the check-out. I noticed a very pale little man (got you guessing?) travelling on the parallel stairway, but going in the same direction! He was very keen to talk to me. Just imagine ever being able to hold a conversation under such impossible circumstances! I assumed he was Russian, but he spoke fluent English. However, he was very anxious for me to explain the meaning of the word 'detailed.' I tried to enlighten him through conveying the idea of 'small' by cupping my hands together very tightly and holding them towards him (I appeared to have no shopping bag to get in the way). This movement was obviously not helpful, and he responded with a tiny shrug of impatience. Then, as swift as a flash of lightning, came the all important final gesture as we were nearing the top of the escalator. From inside his jacket he whisked out a picture I knew intimately. It was an enlargement (which he unrolled and leaned over sideways so that I had a clear view of it) of the sepia illustration of Lenin and Gorky that I had cut from the huge

45

book 'A Day in the Life of Soviet Russia,' which some Russophile friends had given me. It showed the two comrades playing chess, with a shadowy Krupskaya looking on maternally from the rear. The peaceful simplicity of the scene had appealed to me above all the lavish and colourful pictures from every part of the Union. I had removed it from a page also depicting one or two other scenes. In short, the one in question, which I still have pinned on my living room mantelpiece, was, in a way, a detail. My little pale plain friend then disappeared, no doubt satisfied that the meaning of his message would come through clearly. But for some moments everything was far from clear. I felt quite staggered, as the whole episode containing so much in so little time, would need to be revolved carefully in my confused mind. Incidentally, his query about the word 'detailed' had automatically suggested 'small' as he intended it should, but I wasn't quick enough to realise the significance of the word as applied to himself.

As crowds of shoppers were checking out, I was alone, but the rest all appeared to be paired off. A mechanical voice explained that, as they left to make for the main exit, the partners must all separate left and right, to meet at the entrance later.

This seemed like another utter absurdity that puzzled me, but there the dream ended, which was a great relief, as my poor brain I felt could take no more. Of course I knew that the whole scenario was the work of the versatile Gerald. The insignificant little man was certainly no funny freak, in spite of his plain exterior. My heart warmed to Gerald, as he was admitting tacitly but freely, that he had been mean and intolerant to men weaker than himself, and defenceless. Later still, it dawned on me that Gerald had actually identified himself as the man on the escalator, which was a tremendous step forward. He no doubt hoped I would recognise him instinctively, but I wasn't that smart. I began to realise that there need be no limit in the spirit world for character appearance and development.

After the flash of enlightenment on my part, it required no great effort to understand the picture incident. Gerald was simply letting me know that he had come to accept the Bolshevik Revolution as a wholly justified stand of the Russian masses against the tyranny of the Tsar and the fabulously rich nobility. The recent collapse of the Soviet Union does not alter the fact that Socialism under the government of true Socialists, can be the only just system throughout the world. Some day it will be given a fair trial, with some of the smaller states (gallant persecuted Cuba the most shining example) already leading the way.

As a kind of 'Amen' to this Dream of Dreams, I must just add that I in no way felt deserted in the end. I didn't actually see the couples split up - in fact I was hardly conscious of them at all. It was unnecessary for Gerald to wait to leave me at the exit. When he vanished along with his picture, his final message was unmistakable. We both heard the mechanical voice assuring all the shoppers that they would meet at the Far End. He was no longer visible to me, but I felt his presence and solemn promise. Yet closely allied to the solemnity lay the sense of fun. I am quite sure now it was their lack of humour which turned him against people like the so-very-earnest Norman Angell. No doubt they would feel equally irritated by his apparent flippancy over serious concerns. It is all a matter of degree and the chemistry of each individual's make-up. It is often difficult for many of us to be tolerant of opposing views. Gerald and I had by now reached such an advanced state of understanding and unspoken devotion, that no more inter-world contacts would be necessary.

I still had much to do in perhaps a very short time, and we had learned to trust each other implicitly. For the first time I had actually heard his voice and seen his face, albeit most effectively disguised; and his sense of fun, never far below the surface, had been a great help even to my understanding of his serious hidden depths. Most certainly we shall meet at the Far End, the deviations of the past recognised as being due to immaturity and misunderstanding. The 'Far End' for me will mean a 'New Beginning,' with every opportunity for unlimited development, with help and guidance from kindred spirits.

Even more do I look forward to using my reinforced earthly gifts in loving service to children tragically cut off from earthly life and still in the process of growing up. The adaptation problems will not always be easy for any of us, but with mutual love and friendship, happiness will be achieved, helped on enormously by shared fun and humour. But for those not willing to learn, they will find life in another dimension not to their selfish liking. There will be no rewards for the good in heaven or punishments for the bad in hell, but still the opportunity to choose to advance or remain in varying degrees of misery will persist until the daylight begins to dawn. For many of those regarded as particularly clever during their life on earth, but who misused their brain power, they will find the lessons to be learned as particularly difficult.

Chapter Nine

LINKS BETWEEN THE PAST & THE FUTURE

It is now Christmas time, and I feel compelled to close my remarks on 1993 as the end of Part One of this disorientated and disjointed saga. It may be helpful for me to glance backward in order to understand the trend of events leading to the present. But what of the future, unpredictable to a large extent, yet inevitably 'coming events cast their shadows before.' Human life ahead, with its strange blend of chance and influence, can be both fascinating and frightening.

Gerald approached early middle age with loathing, and what would seem an almost cowardly obsession. But suddenly I am pulled up by the recollection that he was not to survive that dreaded period. Intuition may have taken him unawares. Whether he actually sensed an early death can only be conjecture on our part. However, ample proof lay ahead that he was to develop remarkable powers of mediumship. This will be clearly shown later by the unfolding of the novel 'Lover at Forty'; still I will attempt to retain a balance of 'sanity', by introducing some typical examples of his humour, though not always free from touches of malice, as he readily admits.

PART TWO

Chapter Ten

GERALD & SIR EDWARD

I begin this toward the end of New Year's Day as planned. Gerald's influence on the strange devious route of Part One as it developed, was very strong. I am determined to complete its sequel in a shorter time, but I am afraid the order will prove even more disorderly.

First I must make a great effort to set aside the 'Malice' reminiscences as quickly as possible. I realised that he had developed very remarkable powers of clairvoyance in the spirit world. But I must not enlarge on that just now. With relief I came to the end of his Chapter Six on 'Some Writers.' It had begun amusingly enough with the account of an interview with Arnold Bennett, which could be included in the 'malicious' category. A brilliant little sketch of the entertaining character G.K. Chesterton followed as a welcome contrast. As for the other characters, Gerald would have been well advised to ignore them. He was at his worst trying in a nutshell to bring people to life who didn't really live for him. However, writing was his livelihood, and it must be very difficult to dispense with padding altogether.

The succeeding chapter on Sir Edward Elgar on the contrary, must have provided Gerald with enormous satisfaction. As with G.B. Shaw he was privileged to have an invitation to the great man's home. The chief difference between his two hosts, as hosts, was that Elgar proved to be susceptible to flattery, whereas Shaw had no need of it, as all who ever met him must have been well aware. After a preliminary brief encounter with Elgar in Manchester's Midland Hotel, Gerald wrote an 'impressionistic sketch' of him, but remembered nothing of it except his use of the word 'aristocratic' in describing his general bearing. That was enough to persuade Elgar to lift the ban on his ever being interviewed for the Press. And so, a cordial letter of invitation was written by Lady Elgar from Plas Gwyn, Hereford, and Gerald arrived during Christmas week in the throes of a General Election. During the meal, the conversation not unnaturally turned to Politics. After my former little disagreements with Gerald, sharp but fortunately short, I will quote with pleasure his sardonic account of Lady Elgar's strong right wing views.

"I quickly discovered that to confess myself a Radical would be to arouse feelings of hostility in her bosom. Radicals were The Unspeakable People. There was not one, I gathered, in Hereford. They appeared to infest Lancashire, and some had been heard of in Wales. Also, there were people called Nonconformists. Many persons were Radicals, many Nonconformists; but some were both. The Radicals had won several seats. What was the country coming to? Where was the country going? Where, indeed? I did not allow Lady Elgar's rather violent political prejudices to interfere with my appetite, and she appeared to be perfectly satisfied with an occasional sudden lift of my eyebrows, and such ejaculations as: 'Oh, quite! Quite!', 'Most Assuredly!' and 'Incredible.' If she thought about me at all - and I am persuaded she did not - she must have believed me also to be a Tory. After all, had not I called her husband 'aristocratic' and is that the sort of word used by a Radical save in contempt?"

Like his earlier notable host, Shaw, Elgar took Gerald for a walk, but the ensuing conversation bore no resemblance. Elgar for a time was 'reserved and non-committal'. Gerald realised that he must "rigidly abstain from direct questions if he were to succeed in obtaining his views on any matter of interest." He and Ernest Newman had been close friends until the latter felt obliged to criticise unfavourably 'The Apostles.' That severed their friendship for a time, and it was during this hiatus that Gerald made his visit to Elgar. As he particularly desired to induce the composer to throw light on the subject, Gerald ventured to mention musical criticism in general. Not surprisingly, with 'The Apostles' in mind, the subject of religion eventually emerged. It might have been wiser for Gerald to avoid all reference to Newman, an atheist like himself; but as usual, he preferred rather to tread a path of possible thorns, and so he deliberately made a special mention of Newman. I will quote the sentence which indicates plainly his high regard for the critic, and so naturally explains his determination not to allow him to be excluded from the discussion.

"Newman, it is generally agreed, is unquestionably the most brilliant, the fairest-minded and the most courageous writer on music in England. His power is very great, and he has done more to educate public opinion on musical matters than any other man." Elgar remarked later 'He is an unbeliever, and therefore cannot understand religious music - music that is at once reverential, mystical and devout.' 'Devout?' whispered I to myself. Aloud I said: "A man's reason, I think, may reject a religion, though his emotional nature may be susceptible to its slightest appeal."

Then followed a friendly argument about the merits and demerits of programme music, but the friendly tone had a sting in its tail. Gerald skilfully managed to bring Richard Strauss into the picture, concluding (maliciously?):

55

"Strauss who, of all living musicians, is the greatest."

Well, if Gerald wasn't being quite malicious, it was at least 'naughty' of him. I can readily forgive that lapse, being a great lover of Strauss myself, but he deserves censure for deliberately provoking his host further. He continued.

"I represented a Labour paper, but Elgar did not know that I was at the same time writing leading articles for a London Conservative daily. He treated me with the most careful kindness, that might be called patronising. As he, the aristocrat, was in contact with me, the plebeian, it was his manifest duty to help me along the upward path. I was advised to read Shakespeare.
'Shakespeare' said he, 'frees the mind. You, as a journalist, will find him useful in so far as a close study of his works will purify your style and enlarge your vocabulary.'
'Which of the plays would you advise me to read?' I asked with simulated innocence, and playing up to him with eyes and voice.

If only he had been satisfied to continue in similar vein just a little longer, it would have provided a fair example of his ability to amuse by clever, but harmless criticism of an older man's weaknesses. But he was not satisfied until he had dealt the final coup, by praising the:

"beautifully clean and strong English of 'Moll Flanders'."

Elgar, naturally, was not acquainted with 'Moll' so it was left to Gerald to 'enlighten' him with the blunt truth of her profession.

"And that, of course, put an end to our conversation. I rose to leave."

Why must Gerald overstep the bounds once more? Is he trying just to live up (or rather down) to the title he had, unfortunately for himself, chosen for his book. I must admit that in his later book, he is unstinting in his expression of admiration for Elgar, both as a great composer and a fine human being.

Chapter Eleven

TWO BOYS ON A QUEST

In my haste to turn my back finally on 'Set Down in Malice' I shall skip many chapters altogether. However I cannot resist mentioning one incident from Gerald's late boyhood, simply because it throws a little light on another member of his family. In the last of his three chapters all named 'Miscellaneous' he writes:

"Emil Sauer had, fifteen years ago, a technique that no word but rapacious accurately describes. The piano recital he gave in Manchester nearly two decades ago was the first recital I ever attended, though I was a lad in my late teens; the occasion then seemed, and still seems, most romantic. It is true that, on the nursery piano at home, one of my elder brothers used to give recitals with me as sole auditor, and that I used to return the compliment the following evening; but though we took these affairs very seriously, and even wrote lengthy criticisms of each other's playing, our performances were not of a high order. But one evening, defying parental authority and risking paternal anger, we slipped unseen from home and went to hear Sauer. I think we must both have seemed much younger than the average educated boy of eighteen or nineteen today and we were in a very high state of nervous excitement as we sat in the gallery of the Free Trade Hall waiting for the great man's appearance. His slim and, as it seemed at the time, spirit-like figure passed across the platform to the piano, and two hours of pure trance-like joy began for at least a couple of his listeners. My brother and I knew all there was to know about the great pianists of the past, and often we had tried to imagine what their playing was like; but neither he nor I had conceived that anything could be so gorgeous as what we now heard. For once, realisation was many more times finer than anticipation. Only one thing disturbed my complete happiness - and that was the notion that the pianist might possibly be disappointed with the amount of applause he was receiving, though, of a truth, he was receiving a great deal of applause. So I clapped my hands and stamped my feet as hard and as long as possible. The Appassionata Sonata almost frenzied me, and a Liszt Rhapsody was like heady wine.

But all beautiful things come to a close, and towards ten o'clock my brother and I found ourselves on the wet pavement outside, feeling very exalted but at the same time uncertain whether we had done our utmost to make Sauer's welcome all that we thought it should have been.

'Let's wait for him outside the platform entrance and cheer him when he comes out,' suggested my brother. Very strange must that two-voiced cheer have sounded to Sauer as, in the dark street he stepped quickly into his cab, which began immediately to move away. As one voice died, he opened the window and leaned out, holding out to us his long-fingered hand. Running eagerly to him, we clasped his hand in turn, and, amazed, listened to the few words of thanks he shouted to us.

For long after that, Sauer was one of our major gods, and we followed his triumphs both in England and on the Continent with the utmost interest and excitement. When we boasted to our friends that we had shaken hands with the great pianist, they evinced little interest in the matter. 'Why, that's nothing!' exclaimed a Philistine; 'Last Saturday afternoon I touched the sleeve of Jim Valentine's coat!' Now, Jim Valentine was a great rugger player."

Incidentally, the brother enthusiast was not Bill, the eldest, who only seemed to haunt Music Halls. I feel sad to recall that the middle one, so much in tune with Gerald in his musical tastes and talents failed to achieve his potential. He too had a gift for writing, and for a time made a living by turning out serialised romances for the Press. He apparently had high-flying ideas, but lacked the stability of character necessary to succeed. It is easy to censure, but right now I can feel only compassion and sadness that he took the wrong turning. I never heard about his ultimate fate.

Chapter Twelve

CATHEDRAL MUSIC FESTIVALS

I will quote at length from this chapter, as it appeals to me personally, and where I feel at one with Gerald most of the time. Here he writes as you would expect him to talk in a relaxed, almost holiday atmosphere.

"No, I'm not going to be a chronicler, but many things happened in Gloucester, Hereford and Worcester that were vastly amusing and which were not reported in the papers, and it is about these I am going to tell you. It used to be very charming to go to one of these cathedrals early each autumn, drink cider, listen to music six hours a day, walk by the river, have jolly 'rags' in the hotel at night, and come home again at the end of a week or ten days. Everybody used to migrate to these festivals. Well, not quite everybody, but the very people you most awfully wanted to meet again and talk to and hear music with. London used to send thirty or forty critics, and the provinces about the same number. It was hard for us musical critics to take these festivals quite as seriously as the festivals expected us to do, for it always seemed incredible to us that London or Birmingham or Glasgow should have the least desire to know how the choruses of Handel's 'The Messiah' were sung in a little town like Gloucester. Moreover, many of us were amused at the tragic seriousness of these age-old festivals - festivals at which, as a rule, only two new works of any importance were produced, and over which old oratorios

- an impossible form of art - hung like a heavy cloud. So we used to amuse ourselves in our different ways, and the ringleaders in our occasional rags were generally Granville Bantock and Ernest Newman."

I find I must cut out a great deal after all, including the hilarious incident with Bantock's live eels. The fine character of Samuel Langford I find irresistible, and it is a pleasure to introduce him, a complete contrast to Frank Harris, as one really worthy of Gerald's high regard.

"Langford's mind is spacious, most richly stored. Nothing can happen that does not at once and without effort fit into his philosophy of life, and though his talk is profound, it is so greatly human that, in listening to him, one feels completely at rest. Langford will never be 'successful' in the worldly sense. Perhaps he looks with suspicion on success; certainly he has never attempted to achieve it.

It was these refreshing talks with various people that did something to mitigate the severity of the atmosphere of conventionality, that made it rather difficult to breathe freely in these cathedral cities. Everyone wore new clothes; men perspired in kid gloves; girls carried prayer-books and copies of Elijah; deans were dapper; ostlers were clean and profoundly polite. There was too, about these festivals, an air of a society function. Music, an unwilling handmaid of charity, was 'indulged' in.

There is no doubt that our most ecstatic moments at the Festivals were supplied by Wagner's 'Parsifal', which G.F. Runciman describes as 'this disastrous and evil opera'. Only excerpts from it were given; all 'objectionable lines' were cut out. It used to be so fine to come forth from the Cathedral at noon, step into that mellow September English sunshine which I had not seen for nearly three years, and walk by the river and come back to the hotel to eat cool meats and cool salads and drink cool wine. It was at these times I used to long for Bayreuth and wonder if I should ever see the grave of Wagner in the little Bavarian town."

I Sense again his dread of approaching middle-age.

Anti-Climax (Birds Of A Feather)
By Gerald (my short comment at the end)

"Can you recall the most curious and most unlikely sight you have ever witnessed? Of all the strange things I have stumbled across nothing has been so fundamentally silly, as the forty organists I saw sitting in one room at Worcester. One can imagine two, or even three, organists sitting talking together, but forty, and fifteen of them Cathedral organists, seems incredible. Now, you have only to be fond of modern music to feel instinctively that a man who is an organist and nothing else is sitting on the wrong side of the fence. In ninety-nine cases out of a hundred he is helping to hold things back; he hates the rapid progress which music is making, and he has as much imagination as the vox humana stop. Well, the forty organists were sitting and talking and smoking, and as I looked at them and at their mild, but worried, faces, it seemed to me and my companion that, in the interests of art, morality and ordinary decency, some protest should be made. And we decided that we were just the people to make it. We could have forgiven them if they had met together to discuss some professional question, eg. how to get their salaries raised, how to get the better of their respective vicars, or how they could expand their minds so as to be able to appreciate Debussy or Ravel.

But they were gathered together merely because they liked it, just for the sake of enjoying each other's society. Monstrous absurdity! Could they not see how ridiculous they were? Forty organists in one room! - why, there ought not to be forty organists in the whole world. Fortunately the room was on the ground floor and the hour late.

We stepped outside the hotel, waited till the street was quiet, and then rapped a series of three tattoos upon the window-pane to secure silence within. We then sang in two parts, I in a high falsetto, and my friend in a lugubrious bass, the 'Baal' Chorus from Elijah:

'Baal, we cry to thee!
Baal, we cry to thee!'

We had not proceeded very far in this beautiful music intended by Mendelssohn for a shout of savagery, but really a quite charming cradle song - when a cry of delighted laughter came from the room, and two or three of the organists, hatless and earnest, rushed out into the street.

'Come inside!' they said; 'come and join us. You belong to us!' Too utterly flabbergasted at this invitation to make any reply, we turned and fled, rushed back to our hotel, and ordered whisky-and-sodas. The great musician to whom we told the story next day said: 'Well, once more, you see, the biters were bit.' But my friend did not think so."

I suspect a degree of exaggeration in the story, which is a good example of Gerald's malicious fun at the expense of a sect of men harmlessly enjoying themselves in their own way. Perhaps it was an unconscious childish reaction on his part to the threat of creeping age. The stupid over-reaction would meet with my wholehearted opposition but for the fact that his dislike of organ music finds me in wholehearted agreement!

Chapter Thirteen

KARL KLINDWORTH
From the chapter 'Berlin and Some of its People.'

I have chosen to concentrate on one German character only, partly because of his tremendous adoration for Wagner, but even more because of Gerald's inspired description of the old man Karl Klindworth himself. He was writing about the pre-1914 war period, which is not easy for our generation to imagine, even for oldsters like myself. Gerald was in the company of Frederick Dawson, a famous English pianist, who had planned to give two recitals in Berlin. They were staying in a hotel where Klindworth had engaged for Dawson a large room containing a good piano. After leading us up to expect a thoroughly distasteful picture of the city, Gerald still startles us with the strong affirmative sentence:

"A beastly city was Berlin. And yet not all of Berlin was beastly. But the artistic, the musical, part of it was very low. But Karl Klindworth had nothing of beastliness in him. In writing about him I shall feel rather old, and you, when reading about him, will I greatly fear, also feel rather old. You see, Klindworth belongs so awfully to the past. Yet he was a very great man in his day, and there must be still in London many people who knew him in those silly, savage days when stupid people (and they were brutally stupid) thought of Wagner what brutally stupid people think to-day of Richard Strauss. Klindworth was not only a disciple of Wagner's but he was also one of

Wagner's prophets; a forerunner. A great pianist also; a great
conductor; a great man. Frederick Dawson, one of the most
generous-hearted of men, took me to Klindworth's, and said
some jolly, flattering things about me to the great musician.
Klindworth was very old, about eighty years, and, when he
spoke, it was like listening to the voice of a man who had just
got beyond the grave and was not unhappy there. I egged him
on to speak of Wagner. 'What can I say?' he mused. 'Nothing.
Wagner was from God.' His large eyes, two great ponds of
colour in a face not white but stained with ivory, smouldered
and suddenly burst into flame. His hands, always trembling a
little, now shook rather violently. I could not help feeling, as I
gazed upon this old man, that Wagner lived in him as strongly
as he lives in the mighty scores of 'Die Meistersinger' and
'Tristan and Isolde'. We sat silent.
Frau Klindworth, an Englishwoman speaking English most
charmingly with a foreign accent, folded her hands and gave a
little sigh. Dawson shot me a significant look which meant:
'Keep quiet; if you do, he will begin to talk.'
'No one,' said he, 'who was a gentleman, I mean no one who
had ordinary feelings of chivalry, could meet Wagner without
feeling that he was in the presence of one of the Kings of our
world. Certain people, both in England and Germany, have
written stupid things of him; they have pointed fingers at his
faults, banged their fists upon his sins. I hate those people.
Faults and sins? Who has not faults? Who has not committed
sins? You English have a word 'uncanny.' Or is it you Scottish
people? Wagner was uncanny. He dived into things. Yes, he
dived. And every time he lost his body in the blue sea, he
brought back a pearl. A pearl? No; pearls have no mystery. He
brought back, each time, a hitherto undiscovered gem.'
His old mind, outworn and very weary, appeared to cease its
functioning. He sat with no sign of life in him. It was as though
a clock had stopped, as though a light had gone out. And then,

without any apparent cause, he came to life again. 'Let us go to the piano' he said, rising. So we left the little room in which we were sitting and moved to the large music-room, at the far end of which was a grand piano. Frau Klindworth, Dawson and I sat in the semi-darkness near the door; Klindworth's tall but rather shrunken figure moved down the room to the little light that hung above the keyboard. He played some almost unknown pieces of Liszt, interpreting them in a style at once noble and half-ruined. The excitement of playing seemed to increase rather than add strength to his physical weakness, and many wrong notes were struck. It was very pathetic to see this old man trying to revive the fires within him, trying and failing; and I felt that if the ashes of long-spent fires had indeed broken into hot flame, his frail body would have been consumed.

He gave me his photograph and wrote on the back some message, and when I left him I thought I should never see him again. But, a few days later I saw him in the front row of one of Frederick Dawson's recitals, and I occasionally heard from him a deep-noted 'Bravo!' as Dawson electrified us with one of his stupendous performances. Klindworth lingered on for some years later, and when I was in Macedonia last year, I saw in some newspaper a few lines recording his death. In the seventies he was a great figure in London, and Wagner worshippers of those days worshipped Klindworth also, not only for his genius, but also for his loyalty, his noble-mindedness, his devotion to his art."

Chapter Fourteen

RICHTER & THE GERMAN ELEMENT IN MANCHESTER

In my less than headlong dash to escape from 'Malice to Friendship,' I have again chosen to concentrate on a single personality, but this time from a more cosmopolitan medley. It just so happens that another German musician has reared his head. Hans Richter was not a favourite character of Gerald's, but he refuses to be ignored nevertheless. It was his years as conductor of the Halle Orchestra in Manchester that attracted my special attention. I will now begin to quote from Gerald's assessment.

"Hans Richter was an autocrat, a tyrant. During the years he conducted in Manchester, he did much splendid work, but it may well be questioned if, on the whole, his influence was beneficial to Manchester citizens. He was so tremendously German! So tremendously German indeed, that he refused to recognise that there was any other than Teutonic music in the world. His intellect had stopped at Wagner. At middle age his mind had suddenly become set, and he looked with contempt at all Italian and French music, refusing also to see any merit in most of the very fine music that, during the last twenty years, has been written by British composers.
He irked the younger and more turbulent spirits in Manchester, and we were constantly attacking him in the Press. But with no effect. Richter was like that. He ignored attacks. He was

arrogant and spoiled and bad-tempered. 'Why don't you occasionally give us some French music at your concerts?' he was asked. 'French music?' he roared, 'there is no French music.' And certainly, whenever he tried to play even Berlioz, one could see that he did not regard his work as music. And he conducted Debussy, so to speak, with his fists.

Young British musicians used to send him their compositions to read, but the parcels would come back, weeks later, unread and unopened. His mind never inquired. His intellect lay indolent and half-asleep on a bed of spiritual down. And the thousands of musical Germans in Manchester treated him so like a god that in course of time he came to believe he was a god. His manners were execrable. One occasion, he bore down on me in a corridor at the back of the platform in the Free Trade Hall. I stood on one side to allow him to pass, but Richter was very wide and the corridor very narrow. Breathing heavily, he kept his place in the middle of the passage.... I felt the impact of a mountain of fat and heard a snort as he brushed past me. Everyone was afraid of him. Even famous musicians trembled in his presence. I remember dining with one of the most eminent of living pianists at a restaurant where, at a table close at hand, Richter also was dining. The previous evening he had conducted at a concert at which the pianist had played, and the great conductor had praised my friend in enthusiastic terms; moreover they had met before on several occasions. 'I'll go and have a word with the Old Man, if you'll excuse me,' said my friend. I watched him go. Smiling a little, ingratiatingly he bowed to Richter, and then bent slightly over the table at which the famous musician was dining alone. Richter took not the slightest notice. My friend, embarrassed, waited a minute or so, and I saw him speaking. But the diner continued dining. Again my friend spoke, and at length Richter looked up and barked three times. Hastily the pianist retreated, and when he had rejoined me, I noticed that he was a little pale and breathless.

'The old pig!' he exclaimed.

'Why, what happened?'

'Didn't you see? First of all he wouldn't take the slightest notice of me or even acknowledge my existence. I spoke to him in English three times before he would answer, and then like the mannerless brute he is, he replied in German.'

'What did he say?'

'How do I know? I don't speak his rotten language. I only know that he was very angry. He was eating slabs of liver sausage. And he spoke right down in his chest.'

He was indeed unapproachable. Of course, he was a marvellous conductor, a conductor of genius; but long before he left Manchester, his powers had begun to fail. For two or three years I made a practice of attending his rehearsals. Nothing will persuade me that in the whole world there is a more depressing spot than the Manchester Free Trade Hall on a winter's morning. I used to sit shivering with my overcoat collar buttoned up. Richter always wore a round black silk cap which made him look like a Greek priest.

He would walk ponderously to the conductor's desk, seize his baton, rattle it against the desk, and begin without a moment's loss of time. Perhaps it was an innocent work like Weber's 'Der Freischutz' overture. This would proceed swimmingly enough for a minute or so, when suddenly one would hear a bark and the music would stop. One could not say that Richter spoke or shouted: he merely made a disagreeable noise. Then, in English most broken, in English utterly smashed, he would correct the mistake, and recommence conducting without loss of a second. He knew his job, he was a great economiser of time, and he was a stern disciplinarian. He could lose his temper easily. He hated those of us who were privileged to attend his rehearsals. He declared, quite unwarrantably, that we talked and disturbed him. But he never appeared to be in the least disturbed by the handful of weary women who, with long brushes, swept the seats and the floor of the hall, raising whirlpools of dust fantastically here and there, and banging doors in beautiful disregard of the Venusberg music and in protest against the exquisite Allegretto from the Seventh Symphony."

I have just re-discovered a tiny German gem for which room must be made.

"Another German - a dry-as-dust individual, who nevertheless comes to life - but life of mere existence.
Egon Petri had phlegm almost British: a real slogger: most uninspired: the possessor of faultless technique: the possessor of a brain that retained everything but expounded nothing. He had business ability and pushed ahead all the time: pushed ahead all the time, but never arrived anywhere. Never will arrive anywhere in particular, except at his own well-cleaned doorstep, where the polished knocker will respond to his carefully gloved hand."

Obviously well-cleaned doorsteps and polished knockers are just as important to Gerald as they are to me! I myself deserve criticism for this quote, as I had never previously even heard of poor Petri, now given no opportunity to defend himself from such calumny. Poor Petri did I say? What about poor Richard Strauss, who for once must give way entirely to a few whose need for notice may be greater than his?

Chapter Fifteen

CHELSEA 'RAGS' (1914 & 1918)

My nature, ever perverse, though unintentionally, compels me first to refer to the earlier (1914) Chelsea rag, as a significant contrast. Those were the days of the happiness, jollity and good companionship of Gerald's cronies prior to the outbreak of war.

"It used to begin as a rumour, a faint stirring and excitement in King's Road, Chelsea. The artist on the top floor had a private income, plus periodical parcels from home: cooked chickens, cakes, crystalised fruits, three bottles of wine, etc. The lady who occupied the studio below announced: 'Clearly a rag is indicated. Ring up Susie, somebody, and fetch Hearn over and Ivan, and let the Cumberlands know; and oh! Hughes, dear little Herbert, lend me your pots and pans and things. And, Warlow, just run round everywhere and tell all the people you meet. Don't forget John, and I think that Dean would like that girl with fuzzy hair. We'll begin at seven. No, we won't: we'll begin now.'
The little party - the nucleus of the much larger party that was to meet there in the evening - drifted downstairs to Hughes's studio where there was a grand piano and a portable harmonium which appeared to belong to no one in particular. Hughes opened his wide windows and began to play. Harry Lowe with his magnificent but untrained voice, appeared dramatically in the doorway and sang 'For he's a Scotsman' to a great tune

devised, invented, composed and arranged by Hughes and Lowe."

That short preliminary must suffice to whet your appetite and imagination. Oh no! I have some notes here of Gerald's that must not be overlooked!

"Hughes was awfully good to me on these occasions, for he would allow me to improvise the music for the dumb charades. As a player of any kind - he is worlds above me. I used to love to invent Eastern Dances a la Bantock, to fit the gyrations of Harry Lowe, or Debussy chords for anything shadowy and sentimental, or chromatic melodies - prolonged and melting things in the 'O Star of Eve' manner - for luscious love scenes or fat bulgy discords when some real tomfoolery was afoot."

Without Gerald's permission I will now make a great leap.

"The evening lapsed into night, and the night into morn, and again we became boisterous and new ideas were put into shape and little tragedies given in the burlesque manner. The resourcefulness of the mimes! The devilishly clever satire! The good spirits that never failed!"

I have committed the unforgivable. I realise too late that most of the middle part I have omitted should never, never have been sacrificed!

"Early in 1918 I was in London for a brief period after an absence from England of more than two years spent in France, Egypt, Greece and Serbia. My health was broken, my spirits were low. The Chelsea people were dispersed! Only Hearn with his lame foot, was left of the men, but several of the women were to be found. Herbert Hughes, by some miracle, was on leave, and he turned up unexpectedly one night at my flat. We talked quickly, laughed a little, had some music, and fell into silence. 'Those days!' said I. 'Yes. Nothing like them will come again. But all of us who remain alive and are still in England must meet. What about next Sunday? We'll meet at Madame's?' (That idea came from Hughes).

Next Sunday there were seven of us to make merry, whereas in former days there were forty or fifty. But we seven were together once more: we who, as it were, had been saved - saved perhaps only temporarily. It is a long studio in which we sit, but screens enclose a piano, the fireplace, a few rugs and chairs and a table. Madame is tall and quiet and distinguished; her light soprano voice conveys an impression of wistfulness, and her personality, full of charm and a sadness that does not conceal her courage, diffuses itself throughout the room. We have met together for a rag, but no one evinces the least desire to indulge in jollity.

Hughes goes to the piano, for a piano always draws him as a magnet draws steel ... He plays French songs very quietly, whilst we sit gazing into the heart of the fire, each with his own thoughts - thoughts of Harry Lowe in Greece, of Gordon Warlow in Mesopotamia, of those who lie dead, of those who have gone to France and never returned. And Madame gently rises and joins Hughes and begins to sing with most alluring grace, things by Hahn, Debussy and Duparc. The music lulls us into a very luxury of sadness, into a mood in which grief loses its edge and sorrow its poignancy.

To me, who have heard no music for two years, her singing is mercilessly beautiful, that my breathing becomes uneven and my eyes wet. And once again I feel that spinal shiver which as a little boy, I used to experience when I heard an anthem by Gounod, or just caught the sound of a military band as it marched down another road.... I never used to run from the house to see the band, for even in those early days I had an intuitive knowledge that beauty is mystery, and that to probe mysteries is to mar, if not altogether to kill beauty.... And to-night, when Madame comes to the end of each song, I do not speak, I scarcely breathe, so fearful am I that the spell may be broken. But something of the spell lasts even when she ceases singing altogether and, looking at my wife, I know that she feels it too - that, indeed all in our little company are quietly happy, more reconciled to all the brutality and ugliness over the sea, than we have been for a long age. We talk in quiet tones about the past, the present and the future, each contributing something to the common stock of conversation. Madame brings us tea and cakes, and we listen to the dim rumour of traffic in Kings Road. And then, not very late, moved by a common impulse, we rise to leave, and talking softly as we go, make our way outside, where, we did in that spot three years ago, say farewell, wondering as we do so what Fate has in store for each of us and whether for one or more of us this is the end of our life in Chelsea - a life in which we have worked hard and played hard, enjoying both work and play, and in which we have been carelessly unmindful of the danger lying in wait for our country."

Gerald probably never realised during the eight remaining years of his life on earth, that the Great War should never, need never, have happened. But he has certainly learned the Truth in the Spirit World - the greatest lesson of all.

Chapter Sixteen

FINAL FAREWELL TO 'MALICE'

I hope this farewell will not prove to be a prolonged agony. With great relief I can ignore the last chapter with impunity. Its title 'Night Clubs' explains all as far as I am concerned. It is true I had taken all Gerald's Bohemian cronies to my heart, if only as an onlooker, but I was never, even in my youth, gregarious. There Gerald and I agree to diverge.

As I reckon we have dealt with a surfeit of musicians (albeit of a bewildering variety) I have chosen three writers from his penultimate chapter 'People I Would Like to Meet.' Characteristically, W.B. Yeats whom Gerald deals with first, I have relegated to the last, not through perversity or personal choice, but I am hoping to persuade him to melt naturally with the opening chapter of 'Friendship' ('The Amazing Dubliners'). Of D.H. Lawrence I will say little.

Gerald always expressed interest in him without any feeling of affinity. I was gratified with his final assessment. This brief quote echoes almost perfectly my own summing-up of the writer:

"Lawrence has an insatiable curiosity about himself, and it seems at times as though he is not anxious to discover or uncover life, but to penetrate to the deeps of his own nature and shout out at the top of his voice what he has found there. In such egoism, there is strength as well as weakness, and the very fault, so grave and so calamitous, that bars him from achieving great work is, nevertheless, an attraction to those who are much intrigued by psychology."

I will just add that I fail to recognise the 'strength,' because egoists to me are always boring. Full Stop.

Hilaire Belloc, my second choice, though for whom I feel no real compatibility, certainly deserves the esteem in which he is held by Gerald. One paragraph I will quote in full, because it portrays the two men so intimately, who nevertheless were never to meet.

"Nearly twenty years have gone since early one spring I walked alone across Devon from Ilfracombe to Exeter and from Exeter to Land's End. I went alone simply because Belloc had walked alone across much of France and Italy, and the spirit of imitation was very strong within me.

I had just read his glorious 'Path to Rome' and I carried a copy of the first edition in my haversack, reading it by the wayside and forgetting my loneliness (for I was many times pathetically lonely) in Belloc's most excellent company. I pondered over the nature of this man for many hours, envying him, and thinking that a man with such great and diverse gifts must be reckoned among the happiest people alive. During the weeks I walked in Devon and Cornwall I copied him as far as I could in the most minute particular. At Clovelly, one golden evening as I stood talking with some tall, Spanish-looking fishermen, I suddenly made up my mind that I would write to him. I do not know what I wrote, but a couple of days later a reply came from him telling me that my letter had given him more pleasure than any of the enthusiastic reviews in the papers. This letter I pasted in my copy of 'the Path to Rome,' and in 1915 a friend begged me to allow him to take it with him to France. He had a copy of his own, but he wished to take mine. That friend (our worship of Belloc was one of the many things we had in common) now

80

lies dead, and I like to think that his comrades buried my precious book with him."

I will also quote Gerald's final short paragraph on Belloc, chiefly because its opening phrase reiterates the theme that never fails to stir the depths of my soul with foreboding.

"Even now, on the borderland of middle age I cannot pick up a new book of Belloc's without a little thrill: he is so clean, so bravely prejudiced, so courageous. He is a lover of wine and beer, of literature, of the Sussex downs, of the great small things of life: a mystic, a man of affairs, a poet. What, indeed, is he not that is fine and noble and free?"

In the chapter 'People I Would Like to Meet,' Gerald begins with W.B. Yeats. Whether coincidental or no, his second book of Reminiscences begins with 'The Amazing Dubliners,' and not surprisingly W.B. Yeats leads the way. It should therefore be interesting to learn how far Gerald's expectations live up (or down) to reality. I will quote the first paragraph:

"I suppose that even the most outrageously sincere of men are to some extent poseurs, if not to themselves, then to other people. The artistic temperament must either attitudinise or die. Posturing is the most delicate, the most dangerous, of all the arts. To pose before others is risky, but to pose before oneself is most hazardous, for no one in the world is so easy to deceive, and so ready to be deceived, as oneself, and to be deluded by a fancy picture that one has drawn and painted in hectic moments, is to appear to the world as a fantastic clown. Deluded thus, it appears to me, is W.B. Yeats. He is, of course, a fine though not a great poet: no reasonable man can question that. And there are lines and verses of his that have become woven into the very texture of my mind. Moreover, I recognise that it is futile to quarrel with a man because he is not other than he is. Yet I do quarrel with him. I remember a photograph of Yeats, wherein he appears conscious of nothing in the world but himself, conscious of nothing but his hair, his eyes, his hands - especially his hands. His fingers are so long that one is surprised that, his palm resting on his knee, they do not reach to the floor. It is, I concede, a human weakness for a man whom Nature has gifted (or do I mean cursed?) with the appearance of a poet, to play up to Nature and help her by delicate titivations. But to do this successfully, one must have an overwhelming personality - a personality like that of Shelley, of Byron, of Swinburne. It is a simple matter to look like a poet, but to impose that look on mankind is given to few. It is not given to W.B. Yeats.

How is it, I wonder that one rather admires AE for believing in the objective existence of strange gods and spirits, and yet despises Yeats for sharing this belief? It is, I think, because one feels AE has a solid, even massive, intellect controlling his fantasy, whereas Yeats' intellect is not distinguished either by subtlety or massiveness. Yeats believes what he wants to believe; AE believes only what he must. Yeats has an incurable aching for the picturesque, and whilst he believes that he is 'helped' by the supernatural, I think that this help is derived from his own imaginings, if indeed the question of 'help' comes in at all.

Why, then, should I wish to meet this man whom, it is clear, I regard as self-deluded and for whom my respect is mingled with a feeling that is not very far removed from dislike? Really, I do not know. I think that perhaps I wish to study at first hand a mind that is so exquisite in its refinement, so sensitive in its moods, so invariably right in its choice of words.

From all the tens of thousands of words that exist, how difficult it is to select the one word that is inevitable! And how slender and fragile a man's work becomes when his mind must perforce invariably pounce upon the one only word! The great writers were not so fastidious. Scott, Byron, Shelley, Keats, Balzac and a hundred others: take, if you wish, any half-dozen words from almost any page of their writings and substitute six others, and what will be lost thereby? Scott and Byron and Balzac, and even Shelley and Keats, have, I think, not more than a hundred or so pages that could not with safety be tampered with in this manner. There is something lily-fingered and, to me, something disagreeable and effeminate in a writer who, at all times and seasons, searches and burrows for the mot juste. I am curious about such writers, curious though I know instinctively that they love letters more than they love life. To me such men are incomprehensible and in them, somewhere, something is wrong. After all I am something of a student of nerve trouble, and perhaps wish to meet Yeats in order to satisfy myself what precisely is lacking in him."

And so at last we really come to the end of Gerald's first book of Reminiscences, with W.B. Yeats the final victim of his malice. It will be refreshing to welcome 'Written in Friendship', where Yeats will be given a chance to redeem himself. At least I can promise you that Gerald will be 'seduced by the music of his voice.'

Chapter Seventeen

WELCOME TO 'WRITTEN IN FRIENDSHIP'
(The Amazing Dubliners)

When writing about Ireland's capital city, we can expect a little more exaggeration even than usual from Gerald, with the humour undiminished. The volume was published in 1923, so the gap of 70 years in Dublin's history should reveal some advances. I will begin by quoting copiously from the first five pages.

"Dublin is the most provincial city in the British Isles, for it commits the cardinal error of attempting to be self sufficient. It has a theatre, a university, a castle, a cathedral, St. Stephen's Green, and many public buildings gutted by the fire that was one of the most inconspicuous features of the rebellion of 1916. Of all these it is proud. It has, in addition, its own publishers, its own magazines and newspapers and bookshops, and its own intellectual life. Concerning these it is stridently conceited. And it has its own 'society,' of which in these days it never speaks. The spirit of Dublin, looking northward, views Belfast with large contempt; for in that Ulster town money not only talks, but rules, whereas in Dublin the poorest man may be, and generally is, a prince - a prince in his own eyes, but only a seeming prince in the eyes of others.
We all despise money. At least the best people do, and it is in Dublin where all the best people live. Now the human mind is capable of many feats of which the metaphysician knows

nothing. It can at once despise money and yet pursue it. And the Dublin mind, once it has determined to hate anything, does so with extreme thoroughness. In the capital of Ireland poverty is a virtue, pauperism a state of blessedness. The man who is successful in business is considered both knave and fool, and the poet who writes mediocre verse is a reverenced genius. So victorious is mind over matter that even the meanest writer obtains a public. A book, just because it is a book, is sacrosanct; the printed page is always astir with genius; above the head of the man with the unwashed neck beat the wings of fame.

Whenever, in hours of boredom, I think of Dublin, I see a thousand men and women writing down words, erasing them, writing them down again and then talking. Talking about themselves.

With hot, eager brains functioning with enormous rapidity, they hurry from house to house, from flat to flat, and talk about that sestet they wrote the month before last, that new rhyme of Achitophel and asphodel that J.K. Stephens - or was it AE? discovered, etc.... Always themselves. H.G. Wells in London is merely H.G. Wells in London - that is to say, he is nobody. But Theodore Dreiser in the States is to them not even Theodore Dreiser in the States: he is not permitted an existence. Ibanez may drive his Four Horsemen through the capitals of the world, but the dust and stir of their hoofs are un-noted in Dublin, and Marcel Proust, Gabriele D'Annunzio and Joseph Conrad catch not any true Irish reader in the golden webs they weave.

Dublin devours her own books and shrugs disdainful shoulders at the books of the outer world; acts her own plays and sighs over the vanished Synge; plays her own music - no, Dublin has no music: never an orchestral concert in that proud city from one year to another. So Edward Martyn rediscovers Palestrina Sunday by Sunday, and the voice of the folk-singer is heard in that land. Dubliners are faithful to their gods, and of their gods W.B. Yeats is the most picturesque. I was sitting one dark

January afternoon in the drawing-room of Miss Maud Gonne whose beauty I found ravaged by a recent sojourn in an English jail - when Yeats was announced. I was a stranger, palpably English, and less palpably (I hope) a journalist. He gazed upon me with the timid eyes of a fairy beholding a faun for the first time, and, very wisely, I thought, sat down with his back to the light, and faced the sofa on which Miss Gonne and I were resting.

'This,' said she, 'is Mr. Cumberland. He's come to Dublin to write about us all.'

Mr. Yeats did not share her enthusiasm. Eyelids with beautiful eyelashes hid his sight, and he bent down and did something to the fire with a poker. Then, assuming an exquisite pose, with his wrist on his knee and one of his famous hands depending therefrom slimly and whitely against the black of his trousers-leg, he began to talk of fays, fairies, folk-lore, Fenians, Phoenix Park, and other things beginning with F. I have heard some famous talkers. I have sat, staggered and open-mouthed, while G.K. Chesterton made double paradoxes; and I have been suitably impressed by Sir Hall Caine announcing the fineness of the day in a voice and manner that suggested he was disclosing the ultimate secret of life: but this was different - different in every way.

He talked neither to nor at me. It was pure monologue; just talk; the best kind of talk; talk for talking's sake. Suddenly, becoming once more aware of my presence, he looked up.

'I thought,' said I, 'of going to the islands in the west.' It is true the thought had only that moment entered my head, but I believed it would please him. It did.

'Do,' said he. 'Do. Go there and be yourself. Strange folk live there, Mr. Cumberland. A man might well secure a shadowy immortality by living for a few weeks among those men and women. If you went there, you would in a short space become a tradition; things you did would be talked about - '

'That,' I interrupted, 'I can well believe.'

'Yes; and as is their way, the folk would weave fantasies about your sayings. Tales would be told, and I dare say songs would be sung. And all that you would have done would have been just to go about your business as any man may do. But a certain largeness - or perhaps I should say intenseness - of manner is required: something vital, yet elusive; above all, something sincere. Yes, you would go for a walk, or, maybe would stand and look at the sea; and that would begin a tale. And when you went back to London there would be in the islands of the west, strange things said of you and your doings. For you would be, as it were, alive in their midst. In half-a-century you would be a figure embedded in our folk-lore, and centuries hence people would still be speaking of you; though in your own land your name would be on the lips of none.'

'A strange people,' said I gravely.

'You are right,' he agreed. 'And a kindly people, a good people. Children they always seem to me - the most delightful people in all the world.' He mused. 'But' he remarked dreamily, 'these are the rains of winter. You must wait till the fine days come.'

'Oh no,' I replied; 'I must go at once. What you have said has fascinated me. I love to think that in AD 2120 some German professor may go to those islands and study there and write a learned, but completely unconvincing pamphlet on the great hero Cumberland and all the fine things he said and did two hundred years ago.'

He gazed at me earnestly through his pince-nez. 'Stranger things even than that have happened. For example - '

I shall always regret most bitterly that I did not listen to the story that followed.

But the truth is, I was so closely occupied in studying his personality, that I heard here and there only a phrase. Besides, I was seduced by the music of his voice. Never had I heard a human voice so perfectly cadenced, so exquisitely modulated.

Its tone was round and full, its timbre most sweet; and it suggested the gentlest of gentle melancholies. 'How splendidly he does it!' I said to myself as I listened. 'How perfect and complete the pose! Years of assiduous practice have gone to the making of this so delicate work of art.' But a few minutes later I surrendered myself completely to him, and vowed again that never would I, even secretly to myself, accuse him of insincerity, of acting, of seeking to make an impression. Time has turned him into the elf he copies. He is a little more than human. One very early morn fifty years ago the fairies gathered about his cradle."

And so, with all malice forgotten I am delighted to report, I will round off the Irish human fairy tale of W.B. Yeats. By so doing I will have completed the link between the two volumes of Reminiscences.

'Written in Friendship' is waiting for my attention, but this time I must be utterly ruthless with the scissors, for the 'Lover at Forty' cannot be denied the final pride of place. Originally I planned to wedge him between the Reminiscences, but later realised those two could not be treated separately, so hopelessly had Gerald mixed their contents in his crucible. Reluctantly for a start I will eliminate all the other Irish writers and artists, even Gerald's favourite George Russell (AE). Sadly, though I must record his final verdict on the gathering he met at Russell's home:

"They argued not to track Truth to her lair, but to disclose their own smartness."

He made an exception of Russell, and Shaw of course had been dealt with long ago. Do I detect a slight sign of Malice creeping back? My one lament to express before we leave Dublin - that Gerald did not live to see the rise of the Great O'Casey.

Chapter Eighteen

A TYPICAL TIME WARP

It will have been noted that Gerald gave one of his rare indications of his age when fantasising with Yeats. He visualised a fictional German in AD 2120 writing about Cumberland's heroic deeds 'two hundred years ago.' So, he had actually reached the dreaded age of forty. After ruthlessly cutting out Chapter Two altogether I pass on to his introduction to Rutland Boughton who became one of his firmest friends around 1908. Boughton was an interesting character in his own right, but I mention him now mainly because he is partly caught up in a few slight references to Gerald's private life. Incidentally 1908 was the year of my birth when Gerald would be twenty eight. I am getting used to his time warps, which I have easily come to understand, and they need no apology. Later on he met Boughton in Derbyshire, then at his own home in Manchester (probably Withington which is mentioned elsewhere).

Then, when he removed to London, Boughton settled within a stone's throw of his flat in Battersea.

The disruption of the war years followed. Later (a vague hint suggests about 1920) the two friends came together again, and I will quote part of a paragraph that is of great interest to me, although so much has been omitted, for which I have no regrets, as I feel great admiration for Gerald's reticence at such a time.

"I was able to visit Boughton at his school. I found him in difficulties: the times were adverse: there was no prospect of an adequate public performance of any of his operas. But there was no ebbing of his own enthusiasm. I myself was deeply afflicted at that time, but Boughton's personality, his work and the atmosphere of music in which we lived soon brought healing..."

I intended to end on that more pleasing note, with no family details to follow, but Gerald's appreciation of his friend's personality and home is expressed so beautifully that it must find a place.
Now in his early forties and far removed from the brash errors of youth and one or two misguided influences, he provides us with a touching contrast.

"It needs an abler pen than mine to describe the happiness and the fellowship that filled his home with his charming children, and he himself a child among children. During the long winter evenings half-a-dozen of us would sit round the fire and sing catches, glees, part-songs. During the day there was work in plenty. But Boughton is not perfect. His greatest faults are impulsiveness, a too reckless generosity, and a not too wise judgement in his estimates of his fellows. His temper is far from even. I have seen him blaze up in unaccountable anger; I admit, however, that his anger is short-lived and always openly regretted. He is intolerant; but that is no fault, for he is intolerant of intolerable things. He has no belief in half measures, no compromise. He is a faithful hater: no man could love his art and his fellows so devotedly as he if he had not a fine gift for hatred of humbug, cruelty, and all the pretentiousness that (more than the indifference of the ignorant), suffocates so much of artistic endeavour."

A few years only remained for Gerald in this world. I have heard so little of his decline that I will leave his evening time in the shadows, hoping the end was painless and with the solace of close friends. The best was to follow - a new young life of joys and amazing opportunities to learn the secrets that had been veiled.

PART THREE

Chapter Nineteen

THE MODERN NOVEL (January 1944)

I have been able, with much satisfaction, to cut out a great deal from the first half of 'Written in Friendship.' I am trying very hard to concentrate on the parts (often brief) that indicate definite similarities between us, of any kind whatever. However, I will find it impossible to omit extracts that have a special appeal for me, regardless, especially those with a humorous tendency. In his chapter 'Some Considerations of The Modern Novel' Gerald shows a very positive outlook. This quote I consider to be particularly significant and important.

"Our intellectual being is flooded with new ideas, new concepts. Though it may be true that humanity knows no more to-day about the essentials of our existence - our whence, why and whither - than it did five thousand years ago, yet it does seem to us of this generation that we are, as it were, within sight of the outer threshold of these essentials. The soul of man, looking within itself, has seen something a little; out of this little many theories have evolved, and the novelist, having tested these theories in the light of his own experience, has not hesitated to dramatise them, to make them the basis of his psychology, and with them to rake and sift all the facts that he has garnered concerning the nature of man. Dislike Freud and Jung as we may, the debt of mankind to them is already large, and few novelists of the younger generation are altogether immune from their influence. But it is not only in the world of psychology that we are face to face with new ideas, new knowledge; in almost every branch of life we are rapidly, even feverishly, discarding the used for the unused."

Gerald then deals with the common complaint that modern fiction is too much obsessed with sex. Probably the majority of readers would not support such complaints, and after all, the majority of novelists aim to give their readers what they want, so their books have a ready sale which is what the authors want - therefore satisfaction all round, if not intellectual elevation!

"Nevertheless," comments Gerald, "many intelligent people do feel that many of our 'cleverer' novelists are exclusively preoccupied with sex for its own sake, and, resenting this, they cry out for an ampler horizon, a freer air. They are right so to cry. The great novelists of the world have rarely been obsessed by anything save by life itself. And very rarely have they been 'clever'. Mere cleverness runs to exclusive preoccupations, to morbid gloatings, to specialised study. I do not condemn cleverness; I merely remark that cleverness is only cleverness. Brains were never cheaper then they are today, and it is a profound error to confuse cleverness with genius. In intellectual and spiritual greatness, cleverness is taken for granted and is never remarked upon; we do not think of that quality in considering the work of the great Victorians."

Well I partly agree with Gerald, although my intellect could never have previously delved so deeply into the fashioning of a great novel. Of the Victorians I revered George Eliot above all mainly because I admired her outstanding courage and humanity, the warmth of her personality shining through her works. She was not just what some would deride as a reformer, but aimed to uplift the spirits of the downtrodden masses. All this would have fallen flat but for her great gift of humour, at her best when ridiculing the pompous and those who had not time to be happy because over-concerned with trivial self-inflicted household chores - for example women hell bent on keeping up appearances at all costs. Yet George Eliot like Dickens and the majority of Victorian novelists could, at times be too verbose. However that was the fashion. All other things being equal, I prefer word-economisers like many of their successors, with favourites of mine - Daphne du Maurier and Gerald Cumberland showing the way! At this point I must admit to having read only one serious novel by Gerald - 'A Lover at Forty.' His portrayals of the mother and daughter are masterly, but I don't find Trent quite credible (too creditable?) nor yet young Mordurant, but Sir Rex is as preposterous and absurd as any eccentric that George Eliot could create. The real greatness of Gerald's novel (immured so long) is the story itself - its structure and development. The character portrayal of the girl Avril is uncanny, and extremely interesting, as we are left in some doubt on the last page what she is secretly scheming. As a contrast, as early as Chapter Four, suspense and intense anguish over the fate of Hugh could pierce us readers to the core, although the evidence was plain that it was not love for him that caused it.

Then at the end we are left out on a limb, sure only of Mrs. Colefax's double rejections. We know that Trent will stand firm, but can Mordurant escape from Avril's clutches? He is certainly in deadly peril. One person I have not yet mentioned, the most important of all - Hugh's unborn child, conceived before the end of the first day of the story. Whatever infamy of Avril's may yet confront Trent, he will certainly claim the child and live for it. A most unsatisfactory end, yet perfect in its way. Perhaps one day a sequel will emerge, and all will be revealed. That would ruin everything, unless...

As a relief from such human tensions, I will now quote from a quite mundane paragraph, interesting to me solely because

Gerald's reaction to the topic in question is identical to my own.

"I am continually being amazed by those critics who praise the 'observation' of writers like Zola, Flaubert, George Moore and Arnold Bennett. Let me explain that I do not deny that these novelists were and are 'observers' in the true sense of that much misused term, but I have frequently noticed that they are extolled for that dull and unimaginative observation which employs itself in the conscious or unconscious memorising of all the articles of furniture in a drawing-room, the infinite details of a race-course, or the varied and processional beauties of a sunset. To compile mental catalogues and write them down is not the office of the imaginative writer but of the village chandler. Yet many reviewers are most perversely excited by this mechanical method of observing; they maintain by implication that the finest observer is he who sees and remembers more than other people. The contrary, very frequently, is the case. It is not the quantity, but the quality, of observation that is significant in writing. The true observer is he who sees what is not noticed by others. Moreover, the true observer works not only without effort, but without knowing that he is working. The surface of life engages his interest, but it is what is concealed beneath the surface that excites his power of passionate deduction. The academic mind sees with its eyes; the mind of the artist pierces and transfixes with its intuition."

I could not agree more, although it would not have been in my power to delve "beneath the surface" through any "power of passionate deduction."
Of the writers just mentioned, I confess acquaintance only with Arnold Bennett, on the whole held in high esteem by Gerald. I was so bored with the one novel of his that I struggled through, that I unkindly gave him no second chance.

Since Gerald's time, other authors have become popular in spite of being guilty of "dull and unimaginative observation." One romance in particular that I remember is 'Gone with the Wind.' When the furniture of a room gets in the way of the characters and their actions, it is high time to dispose of the show pieces.

Gerald's 'observation' criticisms were a preliminary to an incident in a Hampstead drawing-room. I would have ignored this, but for the fact that he mentions a physical characteristic that adds yet another resemblance to myself. On being introduced to a stranger, he was asked to sit on a low stool at her feet.

"My body, unfortunately, has no grace, and I felt at a great disadvantage as I sat, my knees hunched on a level with my chin, looking up into her live face with its restless eyes so full of curiosity. It was with horror I discovered I was seated opposite a row of occupied chairs ranged against the wall. My self-consciousness swept over me in a warm wave, and I have no doubt my opening remarks were as futile as my opening remarks are apt to be."

How I sympathise with his predicament! I too lack grace of body and proportion, and when young, suffered from painful self-consciousness as a result. Yet how amusing in retrospection! Gerald was obviously quite popular as a lecturer, but admits to being "congenitally nervous, whose thoughts and words vanish when faced by a crowd." He refers to one literary gathering where he read his lecture, and has also been known to memorise them. Again, he and I suffered mutually from 'congenital' nervousness, allied to our distressing self-consciousness. Yet, from childhood I was in my element acting or singing, as I could thus lose my own identity.

Chapter Twenty

MANCHESTER REVISITED (1923)

As Gerald and I were both Mancunians, I will sift through this chapter for odd remarks contrasting the old city with the new. The gap was a mere ten years, yet he notes, "I found the men and women changed almost beyond recognition." It should be emphasised that just prior to his visit he was living "in a world of bewilderment, of wretched drifting, of inner desolation." I will quote the first paragraph.

"Men, it is said, change their bodies every seven years; they appear very much the same from one seven-year period to another; yet the trillions of cells happily alive in 1916 have died the death by 1923, and other trillions of cells have taken their place. Cities are like men; they change with due regularity; but the alteration they undergo is as apparent as it is real. It is the spirit of the places that changes."

Naturally he makes exceptions of the old cathedral cities.

"In them Old England remains faithful to her traditions, good and bad. In London, though men live their lives hurriedly, and though thought is rapid, social and political change is slow; the Houses of Parliament, vested interests, Buckingham Palace, club life, Mayfair, and the influence of old societies and institutions retard development, and any noticeable movement forward is due largely to the new thought that is poured into the

Metropolis from the universities especially from Cambridge - and from the men of the North and the Midlands.

But in Manchester, where life has much of hardness and crudeness, caused by the close application to commerce, by the continuous manufacture of goods by machinery, and by the proximity of man to the special article by means of which he earns his livelihood, social thought is largely engendered and governed by material things. Social problems and their solution spring from those communities in which life is a contest, and poverty a near neighbour. Hence change here is rapid, for when men suffer either physical privation or spiritual limitation, they will have change, even though the means by which that change is effected entail further suffering.

I found the men and women of my native city changed almost beyond recognition. Its spiritual life was worn down to a feebleness that was almost death. Its one real theatre had collapsed. Instead of plays by writers of genius, there were the incredible movies. In the face of this disgrace, Manchester had made a wan gesture of lamentation, but she had done nothing of a practical nature. A faint sigh occasionally suspires from the Manchester Guardian, and there are still to be found men who voice a bitter regret. But in 1912 so vile a thing could not have been permitted. For ten years ago, Manchester was, in large measure, the city of youth. It was the young men who kept the Gaiety Theatre alive; who sent Richter packing; who introduced, in face of the powerful opposition of the Halle Concerts Society, the music of Debussy, Max Reger, Ravel, Bantock and the host of British composers to whom Teutonic prejudice had refused a hearing. It was the young men who formed the Manchester Musical Society, who wrote plays, who organised the little Swan Club which worked with such extraordinary pertinacity and secrecy to create an ampler intellectual and artistic life. This group of men has vanished. I do not know if there are to-day in Manchester any men to whom things of the spirit are more important than the mere case of circumstance. If there are such, their voice is not heard, and their work is unknown. The Theatre Royal, beloved of Henry Irving, and all the great actors of a past generation, is now devoted to the exploitation of Charlie Chaplin, Douglas Pickford and Mary Fairbanks. Manchester is now the receiving house of Los Angeles. It contains the most sumptuous picture houses in our country. The dark places are thronged night by night.

And in this city, given over to darkness, noise and vulgarity, the Manchester Guardian is issued day by day. Whom does it influence? Not the people. The people know it not. Why should they? For it is devoted to a rather narrow and fastidious intellectuality, far removed from ordinary life. Loving Liberals, it faintly dislikes true liberality. Moreover, it disdains to notice what the man in the street is doing: what the man-in-the-street does in his thousands is not, presumably, now a matter for record, though in the old days it was not unregarded. I went to a Sunday League concert in the Free Trade Hall to hear Frank Mullings sing... Now, when he sings in Manchester, the Manchester Guardian becomes ecstatic: the public is told that he is a great artist, and, on occasions, half-a-column has been scarcely sufficient to hold the news.

But this has happened only when he has appeared at a Halle Concert or at some other gathering of equal social consequence... At the Sunday League concert there were more than three thousand people; at a Halle concert there are never even two thousand; but at the latter are to be found most of the men and women who, heedful of their reputation for 'culture', dare not stay away. Yet, searching the columns of the Manchester Guardian on the morning after Mullings had appeared on Sunday, I found no record of his visit. So far as that paper was concerned, the concert had never taken place. This, of course, is not journalism. It is mere snobbism. A paper that plumes itself on its democratic sympathies and ignores the musical enthusiasm of what, for Manchester, is a very large audience, can scarcely make its influence felt in those directions where liberality of thought and a genuine, broad culture would be most welcomed. One feels, in this newspaper, a straining to catch the attention, not of the population of Manchester, but of extreme intellectuals in Geneva, Berlin, Moscow, Boston, and other places where they sit and think. It is desiccated with thought, and buttressed with the prejudice of a dead generation. It is without passion - sicklied o'er with the pale cast of scrupulosity. And it looks a thousand times before it leaps... and then it does not leap.

The academic and pedantic withdrawal of the Manchester Guardian from the full life of the people coincides with a materialistic decade in which modes of obtaining pleasure - and, indeed, pleasure itself - have sunk to a deplorable level. The war has reduced Manchester to spiritual beggary, and in the time of need, the newspaper that Lord Northcliffe used to declare was 'the best in the world' has forsaken its people and, drawing away its skirts from the contamination of the crowd, has sought refuge in an aridity of soul and a 'politeness' of mind."

Perhaps Gerald's nostalgia and bitter disappointment are partly due to other causes, as the relentless passage of time threatens to overtake him.

Chapter Twenty One

MUSIC IN WALES (1923)

We have already become acquainted with Gerald's uncompromising criticisms of much of the music performed at the Cathedral Festivals. He is equally malicious when reviewing the "enthusiastic Welsh musical gatherings, the National Eisteddfodau." I will omit his scathing remarks about the works of the reverend Joseph Parry, and will be as brief as possible over his prolonged argument with Dr. Macnamara on the subject of Welsh music. This became quite tedious and even embarrassing, so I will select a few extracts only that rise to a higher level.

Dr. Macnamara: "I always advocate the smaller peoples working out their own literary and artistic destiny untroubled by what is being created outside their borders."

Gerald: "That seems to me rather cruel. For you advocate retaining all the barriers that political and social economy, adverse circumstances and nature have already erected between Wales and the outside world. Has England nothing to teach Wales? Has Germany nothing to teach her? - or France?"

Dr. Macnamara: "Plenty, no doubt; but nothing that Wales cannot do without' (looking at me rather fiercely, hostility in his chin, aggressiveness in his splendid shoulders). 'Besides Wales is too small a country to absorb the culture of the entire world. You might as well ask a squirrel to assimilate a granary. Already I am told that Welsh music is dominated by Teutonic influence."

Gerald: "Only the slave is ever dominated. If Wales cannot absorb the culture of the whole world, so much the worse for Wales. I believe she can; and she will begin to do so the moment she recognises that music is not solely an emotional art, but an art demanding rigorous intellectual application. Wales, being isolated, is content to crawl, while the rest of the world is marching forward."

"I am fully persuaded that music in Wales cannot begin to develop until Welshmen free themselves from that intellectual slackness and spiritual fear that find expression in a narrow interpretation of religion, and in a distrust of that natural expansiveness of the soul without which there is no true life. A curious and laughable example of the failure of Welshmen to recognise that music has any meaning but a purely surface one occurred at Ammanford last year (1922). One of the test pieces for soprano soloists was 'Hymn to the Sun' from Rimsky Korsakov's 'The Golden Cockerel'. The song is sung by a young maiden to an old man whom she is anxious to seduce. And seductiveness and sensuousness suspire from the song like mist from a tropic river on a cool evening. There were some thirty competitors in this class-young ladies, musically ambitious, but with unawakened imaginations. Of all the places in Ammanford in which this competition could have been held, a chapel was obviously the least suitable, yet it was a chapel that was chosen for this purpose.
'What', one could imagine the Eisteddfod authorities saying to themselves, 'what a splendid place for a hymn! - the chap-pel!'
So to the chapel I went at nine o'clock one morning to hear this unabashed and pagan music sung innocently and unmeaningly

by thirty of Wales's daughters. My spirit of irony and mockery was delighted by the delicious situation. The music was given with due maidenly reserve, every singer no doubt feeling a Sabbath devoutness as she essayed the melting chromatics... But there was a sequel. Out of the thirty competitors the three best were chosen to sing the same song later in the day in the huge Pavilion when the final adjudication was to be given; before this took place, but at the conclusion of the preliminary test in the chapel, one of the adjudicators explained to all the competitors that each had failed utterly to interpret the song they had sung. He described to them the opera and, in particular, the scene in which the 'Hymn to the Sun' is delivered. With a humour that dared everything he pictured the seductress pleading for love.... Wales's thirty daughters stared in incredulous and shocked amazement.

Could such things be? A few smiled and simpered; most looked stonily and with frank hostility at the adjudicator; only one or two looked intelligent....

Yet, a couple of hours later, when the three chosen ladies appeared in the Pavilion, they altered their tactics; the inhibitions of hymns and chapel associations were cast aside, and Rimsky Korsakov's music was interpreted as he and heaven - for surely this song came from heaven! - intended it to be.

From this little story one knows that the ordinary Welsh singer does not approach his music either with his intellect or his soul, but with the easy emotions that see in melody only melody. But one learns also that this same Welsh singer, if instructed - and shall we say instigated? - can also interpret the spirit that animates melody. Welsh people are not necessarily without imagination, but their imaginations are almost atrophied by fear. They distrust what is beautiful. It is a puritanical distrust - a distrust of what in themselves is noble and free.

It is the custom of the National Eisteddfod to invite a number of English musicians to adjudicate at their meetings. It is a wide-minded policy; or is it a cunning one? At all events, the invited guest, treated royally and paid handsomely, never finds it in his heart to say what he really thinks. He finds, as all visitors must do, a great deal to admire in the musical life of Wales, but he quickly divines the weaknesses of that musical life - its easy and not always sincere emotion, its lack of intellectuality, its meagre aesthetic quality. But he is tongue-tied by the kindness of his hosts; the social relationship between him and the Eisteddfod authorities makes it almost impossible for him to be as intellectually fearless as the musical occasion demands. As a result, he praises what there is to praise, and glosses over the matters that require criticism.

Dr. Henry Coward introduced himself to me at Ammanford. He is, I suppose, the most widely honoured man in Yorkshire: perhaps the most widely honoured musician in the North of England. As a boy he suffered from many of the limitations that adverse circumstance can impose upon talent and ambition. Not until the age of thirty nine did he enter the musical profession, yet if ever there was a man who may be said to have been born a musician, he is that man.

Now, at the age of seventy-three, he has the most delicate ear of any musician I know; its sensitiveness, its power of perception, its ability to separate a single voice from a score of voices is truly extraordinary...

With me it is always an effort, though an intensely pleasurable one, to listen to music; I must concentrate all my faculties in order to receive fully what is being given to me. But Dr. Coward's psychology registers musical impressions as easily and effortlessly as a photographic plate. Sometimes we would carry on a whispered conversation whilst an indifferent choir was singing.

'Here is the prospectus of the Sheffield Musical Union, Mr. Cumberland. You see we are doing.... not quite in the middle of their notes, those sopranos are they? Sharp - a wee bit .... very

varied programmes, I like to be as representative as possible....
Wooden rhythm. There, they quite missed that phrase - all is
tenderness. Flat - the tenors are getting flatter and flatter. The
whole choir's down an eighth of a tone now a quarter. Poor
balance... But we scarcely touch the ultra-moderns. Interesting
men, Stravinsky and Scriabin, but in Sheffield we can't afford
to make experiments. It isn't as if... a semitone down now: a full
semitone, would you believe it? Everything's loose, they don't
hold together. He's trying to rally them now - too late. They'll
never recover themselves.... we had concerts once or twice a
week, and could throw in something very novel occasionally.
We can't do that. It's all a matter of money of course. Most
things are'."

Well, just now I have overstepped the mark!

Chapter Twenty Two

1. LAMENT FOR LOST YOUTH
2 & 3. EMBARRASSING CONTACTS

I hoped to skip over chapter fourteen, but cannot omit two or three gems:

1. "Nothing in life can compensate a man for the loss of the restless dreams of youth. Success in middle age is nothing; it comes too late. And I cannot believe that the solvent years of the fifties and sixties, though they may bring peace and contentment, are worth a single week of the early twenties when the world is wonderful and each hour full of expectancy. For what are the peace and contentment of early age? They are naught save the result of a determination to expect nothing from life.... In old age spring must be pain and autumn a menace."

I could not disagree more - with every word! We are so much alike in so many ways, by nature, but the courses of our lives have been totally different, with probably the male and female distinctions having the paramount conflicting influence. Alternatively it could simply be because Gerald was by nature gregarious, and could not be happy living alone, whereas with me I never felt free in a crowd, or lonely when alone.

Youth of course brought much joy, but even more turmoil and worry. My education left much to be desired, and I was too nervous to assert myself. However the inner spirit of rebellion could never be stifled, and from a very early age I began to doubt generally accepted beliefs, revelling in books that encouraged scepticism. I never shared Gerald's hours "full of expectancy." In fact I learned never to expect great things to happen, because that meant I was saved much bitter disappointment. I admit it was a somewhat negative attitude to life, but I adapted when freedom came in middle age, and I learned to trust myself and develop convictions.

Gerald did not look forward to the peace and contentment of early age. Here we differ profoundly. My form of peace and content is entirely personal, which certainly does not mean I am self-satisfied. I am thankful for good health, and a newly acquired interest in people generally.

Surprisingly though I can now face and enjoy struggles and arguments, all part of the eternal search for the ultimate Truth. But here I am wandering again.

2. Near the end of an interview with General Bramwell Booth, Gerald felt slightly uncomfortable under an unflinching gaze. This reminded him of a much more embarrassing experience.

"I went for treatment to the Coue Institute. At the end of the seance I was asked to close my eyes. When I had done so, a lady began to suggest that from that moment all my bodily organs would function with more and more normality each day: I was told, for example, that my liver would conduct itself with propriety; that my saliva would appear in the right places in due proportions at the correct times: that my heart would beat - well, heartily; that my digestive organs would digest all that was given them for that purpose; and so forth. I remember feeling very apprehensive as her voice went relentlessly on. I trembled at what she might say next. And though my eyes were closed, I felt she was reading my ultimate secret. I blushed painfully, and continued blushing until her words had dealt

with the functions of my knees, my calves, my feet....
But though I did not blush when under the examination of
General Booth's gaze, I felt naked, discovered. He was - I was
sure of it - steadily finding out all I would have no man
discover. I tried to rise, and failed. He held me by his gaze.
'And now, Mr. Cumberland,' he said, after a million eternities
had passed, 'tell me: Have you made your peace with God? Is
everything right with your soul?'
It was not. I told him so; and I tried to say so in a tone of suitable
regret. I informed him that I was not a believer. 'There are so
many intellectual difficulties', I murmured. I felt that this
admission seemed to him boastful, for, on hearing it, he
appeared to lose all interest in my present and future state.
When he had given me his blessing, I left him; before I had
turned he was immersed in his papers: already I was forgotten."

3. I will now add a very contrasting incident related by Gerald,
although equally embarrassing.

"'Plum' Warner sat in a stockbroker's office reading sporting
magazines; as I entered the room he peeped at me over the top
of the page and gave me a shy look. Pulling out a chair, and
seeming more than a little embarrassed, he wished me good-
morning and asked me to sit down. I did not understand his
embarrassment.
It was almost as though he had been taken unawares by, say, a
fulsome flatterer; yet I had not come to flatter, and a short
correspondence and a chat over the telephone had preceded
this interview and invitation to lunch; moreover, I was there
solely on a matter of personal business. For a long time
conversation was almost impossible. Question from me, answer
from him. Then silence. Another question, another answer; a
longer silence. Then, from both of us, unnecessary noises:
coughing, the pushing back of a chair, the tapping of a heel on

the floor. Cigarette? Thanks. I have matches, thank you. More coughing. A restless movement. Gold Flake. Always Gold Flake now - war habit, you know... A terrible silence, this time, it lasts for ever, until, thank Heaven! - the door begins to open! Enters a live stockbroker! Saved! The new-comer wanders aimlessly to the table, stands there a moment deep in thought, looks at but does not see us, pats his under lip with immense deliberation, mutters to himself a vague resolve to have lunch, and disappears.... Jupiter! We are alone once more. It begins all over again. Quite warm for the time of year. January's a funny sort of month. Nice yesterday, though. Still, the day before that was... O vile ineptitudes! I will speak no more.

But to myself I said: 'How very, very different from what I expected!... But then people always are different.' I willed myself to indifference and fell to contemplating his record. Rugby: Captain of the XI, twenty years ago. Three years later Oxford XI. Honours in Final School of Jurisprudence. Yes, of course: a barrister: almost I'd forgotten that. But surely barristers talk? No. Not all. Not this one.... Captain of M.C.C. Team eighteen years ago. South Africa War. Books and journalism.... But so shy and shrinking. Again I heard the silence. It impinged itself upon my every sense.

At last - what the effort cost, I shall never know - he spoke. 'Let's go and have lunch.' It seemed a pearl of wisdom as it dropped from his lips.

Out in the open air he released himself and there began a conversation befitting reasonable beings. He complimented me on a book I had written. 'Most amusing!' he said. He contrived a brief chuckle. But he did not mention the book's title. Somehow or other I gathered that, at the most, he had read only a few pages.

Still, I was grateful. But soon I began to suspect that he was ignorant of my identity, that he believed himself talking not to Gerald Cumberland, but to someone else. But I did not dare to put him right. Moreover, I feared another cloud of embarrassment. But in the crowded restaurant we got on to safer ground - cricket. He had a delightful smile, a good stock of anecdotes, and a real, deep modesty. He took it for granted that he was the most ordinary person in the world. From cricket he went on to golf and tennis. By the end of our meal we were on easy, friendly terms.

On preparing to leave the restaurant, a stranger - a very young man - who had obviously been awaiting his opportunity, approached Warner in something of the manner in which a devotee nears a shrine. He murmured a few words about 'being proud to shake him by the hand', and stood panic-stricken at what he had done. But in a moment Warner had put him at his ease, talking to him with an easy and surprising casualness.... A few days later I received a letter from the Rev. Canon Hannay, 'George A. Birmingham'. It ran thus: 'The enclosed photograph was sent by Mr. P.F. Warner to me, under care of my publishers, addressed with my pen name, 'G.A. Birmingham.' A very nice letter came with it expressing the pleasure Mr. Warner had found in lunching with me the day before, somewhere in the city. As I hadn't been in London since the beginning of December, and had certainly never lunched with Mr. Warner or asked for his photograph, I wrote to ask him what mistake had occurred.

I received in reply another very nice letter from him, explaining that the photograph was meant for you and addressed to G.A. Birmingham through inadvertence. I don't know how he came to make this mistake. It isn't even as if Birmingham were the capital of Cumberland."

117

Chapter Twenty Three

TWO MUSICAL CONDUCTORS

"It can have been a surprise to but few people that Sir Thomas Beecham's services to music had resulted in his financial embarrassment. This was not due to the circumstance that he had conducted thousands of operatic performances without payment, but to the circumstance that both in the metropolis and the provinces he had been inadequately supported by the public. This is our British way of rewarding those who labour for our delight. No one feels any particular responsibility, because the matter is everyone's responsibility. There we have a man who puts his fortune and his genius at the disposal of the public; a man who throughout his career has striven for the highest ideals; who has achieved one artistic triumph after another; who has delved into the literature of music, and unfolded treasures that only learned students of the art knew to be in existence; who has disseminated his culture throughout the land; and who has put new life and a strange ardour into a form of art that, before his appearance, was in danger of sinking into vulgarity and decay. Few of us are in a position to estimate the educational benefit that the country as a whole has gained from his work; but there must be thousands who can individually testify that Sir Thomas has widened their intellectual horizon, refined their perceptions, quickened their imagination, and provided them with abundant aesthetic pleasure. If he had spent himself on the exploitation of 'commercial' music, if he had hired out his genius to the highest bidder and been content to make a compromise with his ideals, England, though losing the benefit of his great culture, would have regarded him with the wholehearted approval inevitably given to the man who seizes the main chance. England understands that kind of conduct. But that a man should devote himself to art and to the education of his generation is the one unbelievable folly, the one unpardonable sin.

But we cannot believe that Sir Thomas Beecham's career will be cut short, though we have no knowledge of how his present difficulties can be surmounted. Such a spirit as his is not to be daunted, for he believes in his cause and must remain faithful to it whether it succeed financially or no. Every other kind of success is already his.

For a long time he must have viewed with equanimity the contempt in which music is held by the vast majority of educated people. That contempt has its roots in the past; it has some kind of historical warrant; but there is no excuse for its survival to-day as a retrogressive and crippling force.

Ignorance may be forgiven, but ignorance that is boastful of itself, that seeks to belittle what is noble, is meanly infamous and past forgiveness."

I felt compelled to quote this eulogy intact, mainly because it gave me enormous pleasure that Gerald should appreciate the genius with such a heartfelt tribute to his selfless determination to devote all his life to the musical service of the public. Any 'malice' was reserved for the undeserving public itself - at least the public of England. I believe that Gerald was not far wrong in his estimate, but being Gerald, I detect a trace of inconsistency and optimism. After all, Beecham's 'new life and ardour' had obviously fired him, when he wrote "a spirit as his is not to be daunted, for he believes in his cause and must remain faithful to it whether it succeed financially or no."

I have headed this chapter 'Two Musical Conductors,' but that

120

was not according to my original plan. As I re-read Gerald's inspiring stimulus, who should suddenly break through uninvited, but our brilliant young north star, Simon Rattle! The cheeky boy's gatecrashing had shown no respect even for Gerald's private domain, but we forgive him unreservedly - in fact we welcome him with open arms. This is no place for me to discuss in Alfred Brendel's words the abilities of 'the most stunningly gifted young conductor I know,' but I will at least comment on aspects of his character which strike me so forcibly as making him a worthy successor of Beecham, another great Merseysider.

Simon, born in 1955, enjoyed a meteoric rise to fame since his early love for the piano, and instinctive ability with his drum! I myself remember with pleasure his first appearance at Liverpool's Philharmonic Hall as a child conductor, when he won the award 'Young Musician of the Year.' In 1973 he made his first appearance as a conductor of the Merseyside Youth Orchestra. He was only about twenty-five when he became the principal conductor to the City of Birmingham Symphony Orchestra. He took over during a difficult crisis, but he gloried in the challenge to build up the orchestra.

The players gave him every support, and years later he signed an agreement to stay with them at least until 1991. He still remains there, in music a cosmopolitan, but never forgetting his roots in the North and Midlands. Even Brummites who are not very musical, took him to their hearts, especially when he resisted even the lucrative offer to forsake them for Los Angeles. I need not stress the parallel with Beecham (both incorruptibles).

Chapter Twenty Four

MUSIC MINUS MUSICIANS

My ideas still refuse to be caged or controlled, and from time to time, insist on wilful wanderings. However, as the saga makes no pretence to be a history, perhaps its untidiness may be excused. The way Simon appeared unceremoniously in the former chapter caused only one more upset apple cart to a whole series. Gerald's chapter following the discourse on Sir Thomas Beecham is headed 'On Musical Conductors,' and I had intended to add brief comments on them with suitable quotations. I have now changed my mind and promise to mention one more conductor only, who was a very popular one, and he will not appear till the end. I will rashly make one more promise, and that is to curtail the rest of the 'Friendship' book with no further mention of music or musicians (sighs of relief?). But the rest of this chapter will be concerned mainly with the subject of 'genius,' which naturally will include composers, along with writers, painters, sculptors, architects and any other occupations you can think of. I will now with relief, let Gerald take over, with his refreshingly clear convictions, minus any named identities.

"It is often asserted that among the large number of excellent musicians in our community there are many potential conductors of first-rate powers whose talents lie hidden through lack of opportunity for their development. In order to conduct there must, it is true, be those who wish to be conducted; without them even a genius must beat the empty air and win no sound. But in this country we have only some half-dozen orchestras that can be regarded as first-rate; there is work then for only half a dozen men." (Gerald names the six, none of whom are still living). "After them comes a host of younger musicians who like to conduct a big orchestra when they get the chance, but whose chief work lies in other directions - composing, teaching, etc. Among these younger men there are, we are asked to believe, interpretative geniuses who will never have a complete opportunity of disclosing that genius. In our musical life there is not room for them. Only large and wealthy cities can continue to keep a full orchestra in existence, for a body of seventy or eighty players is an almost unbelievably expensive organisation. It is not merely a question of money.

A millionaire might conceivably give a series of orchestral concerts in Portsmouth and charge quite reasonable prices, but would he be able to induce the public to attend them? He would not. The concert-room would not be half full, for Portsmouth knows and cares nothing about classical music... A cultured, eager and enthusiastic public must be waiting to hear music before music can be heard. Again, there are the instrumentalists. Where are they to be obtained? Each member of an orchestra like the London Symphony is a highly trained artist, a musician of some scholarship. Such men are not common, and most of them flock to London.

The conductor is faced by a blank wall. He cannot even learn his art, for where is the orchestra on which to practise? It will seem to the unreflecting that the conductor of innate but inexperienced genius is fated to be frustrated all his life. The principles on which our social and artistic life are constructed appear to rule him out. Simply he is not wanted. But, as H.W. Longfellow chants 'All things are not what they seem.' Nor is this. For, if, in these days of uncertainty, there is one thing more certain than another, it is that genius will find a way. There accompanies all artistic genius an intense, unquellable and hungry desire for self-expression. It is a kind of lust of the soul. Just as a river, however much it may meander and turn back in the direction of its source, will inevitably reach the sea, so genius, though it be thwarted a thousand times, will in some way find the means for its consummation. A youthful conductor, lacking an orchestra, will organise one of his own; failing that, he will attach himself to a cinema, or restaurant, or provincial theatre; for, if he have the true gift, he will rather conduct a tenth-rate orchestra of a dozen men than play first fiddle in the London Symphony.

I am old enough to have watched at close quarters, and from their beginnings, the careers of two of our most eminent conductors of the younger generation. With one of these I was on terms of close friendship in his student days. He had great talent and great ambition. At the age of twenty-five, having made a reputation in the provinces as a composer, he came to London with the avowed determination to become a conductor. But he was unknown in the metropolis; he had few friends and no capital; he was doing hack-work of a most soul-destroying kind; his life was as obscure and as unnoticed as that of an ordinary bank clerk; and when he declared to me that before ten years had passed he would be conducting the finest orchestra in the country, his resolve seemed as fantastic and as impossible as if he had told me of his intention to become Prime Minister. Yet well within the time he himself had allotted, he was conducting 'Tristan' and many other operas at Covent Garden under you know who. The truth is, men of genius, whether musical, literary or artistic, do not have anything like so hard a time of it as is generally supposed. Two forces are at work to aid them: their own hunger for power and recognition, and the strong desire of men of established position to discover them. The young man of genius can be bought cheaply and exploited easily; for these reasons he is preferred by publishers, impresarios and agents to men who are already famous. The man of reputation asks and gets a fee that is always enormous and sometimes exorbitant; the beginner, no matter how gifted he may be, will sign any contract that seems to offer him a chance. So that, in these days, there are few (I doubt if there are any) men of genius languishing in undeserved obscurity.

A conductor, to be immediately successful, must, like all artists who appear in person before the public, not only have personality, but he must possess the kind of personality that is readily communicable - that impinges itself directly upon the mind of the beholder. He must have the appearance of being what he really is. Without exception, all the greatest of our European conductors are men of this kind. Sir Henry Wood, chiefly by his Promenade Concerts, has done fine educational work. For many years the man-in-the-street has been able to hear, season by season, the finest classics of the world's musical literature: if any Londoner does not know the nine symphonies of Beethoven, through and through, it is because he does not want to know them."

Chapter Twenty Five

NARRATIVE STRUGGLING FOR COHERENCE

The four remaining chapters of 'Friendship' I approach with sadness, as I sense a vague but disturbing shadow haunting Gerald's closing years. He wisely makes no attempt at continuity. The old spirit of controversy still survives, but I feel that the characteristic sparkle has vanished. He is still capable of stimulating our thoughts and even causing amusement, so I will try to concentrate on the positive aspects. The final chapter is dated 20th May 1923. He died three years later, and I have no real knowledge of that period, nor would I wish to probe into what must have brought much mental as well as physical suffering.

The four chapters I will melt together and try to produce a slightly more satisfactory narrative; for example, Gerald's persistent but vain efforts to make some sense out of spiritualistic phenomena, will be related in my final chapter, obviously the most appropriate place to accompany my own convictions, proven at least to myself. Right now I have no inclination to dwell morbidly on his decline, but rather to stress the ultimate importance of his new life. Perhaps after all, he realised his great mistake while still in his earthly state. I would love to be assured that the end had been peaceful, with faith in the future. From chapter eighteen of 'Friendship' I have chosen two notables only on which to comment. C.R.W. Nevinson is an interesting case. The following character-study attracts me particularly as it throws a new light on Gerald in his post-war maturity, confirming a lament by Neville Cardus that 'he died too young, with his best work still within him.'

"Quick success - success in early youth - is always a handicap. It has weighed heavily on C.R.W. Nevinson. During the war he became famous by bringing a clear eye and an untarnished imagination to the presentation of the horror, pity, courage and drabness of mankind under the scourge of that world-affliction which, to some sentimental minds, is already covered with the glamour of romance. Nevinson's trench pictures are for posterity. To-day they are disregarded because we would forget the things they tell us. They are for posterity because they are true - spiritually true.

In those days Nevinson was something of a rebel. When first I came across him, in the early months of 1919, he was, however, already trimming his sails to catch more prosperous breezes.

He had abundant self-confidence, but he was tired of flouting the Philistines. Self-confident? One might use a harsher term for that flamboyant speech he delivered at the dinner some of his admirers gave in his honour on the eve of his departure for America. It was a clever, muddled, conceited harangue which must have been regretted by all who had his interests at heart. But it was delivered without a single doubt, or a moment's hesitancy.

Self-doubt can, of course, be carried to excess; in moderation, it is a fine purge. And when Nevinson begins to doubt himself he will step on the road to his greatest success. He has views about everything: final views delivered with immense cock-sureness. I have heard him dismiss the sociological and political writing of Wells and Arnold Bennett as 'amateur thinking.' Yet he himself is by no means a correct thinker. He has personality, full-flavoured and strong. And he is a mighty worker. For myself, I admire immensely the artist or writer who begins his work each day at the same hour with the regularity of a bank clerk, and continues it unflaggingly through the four, six or eight hours he has set himself. That is the method pursued by Nevinson when there is sufficient daylight. In the evenings he talks in the Cafe Royal. But in these days there is no talk in the Cafe Royal that is worth listening to. The gaudy place has pleasant associations for many of us, but it has lost its old spirit of ten years ago - its casualness, its brilliance, its unforced Bohemianism. There is a good deal of the visionary in Nevinson. He has the eyes of a mystic. But he lacks the psychologist's gift. The individual man or woman does not interest him. His mind is obsessed by the strange driving forces of human nature, the blind mass-forces that lure the world on to cruelty, to devotion, to self-immolation, to self-aggrandisement. One hesitates to use the much-abused word 'cosmic,' but it best describes Nevinson's passion, half-conscious and as yet hesitant and fumbling, for the good and evil spiritual forces in whose grip humanity is held."

Gerald I owe you an apology, hoping it will be the last. Here is no sign whatever of deterioration of intellect, or brooding obsession with an imminent menacing personal fate.
In fact there is clear indication of increased sensitivity for mankind as a whole, and wisdom developing with maturity. However, I feel just now that a little humour might not go amiss.
The second character that I have picked out of a motley mixture in the same chapter is that of a personage named Walter Winans. I have to admit that I don't remember ever having heard of him before, and from what I have just read, we appear to have nothing in common. Why, then should I have chosen him to accompany Nevinson? The answer is 'just for that very reason, paradoxical as it may seem.'

Even stranger, the incident to be described can even be regarded as one more piece (though a tiny one) for my jig-saw puzzle. I need only add in advance that my attitude to horses is identical with that shown by Gerald.

"Only yesterday it seems that, as I stood in the hall of Surrenden Park, Walter Winans, bearing himself with an air of distinction, put his hand about my elbow, and guided me gently to a room whose furniture, as I remember it, consisted solely of a table laden with every imaginable kind of drink. A magnificent creature with 'fair round belly' waited anxiously to learn my choice. It was a hot summer morning, and I drank from a cut-glass tumbler against whose sides spiky ice clinked deliciously. Winans regarded me solemnly and, the drink finished, said: 'The first drink is good, but I have heard the second is still better.' I made a weak and, I was glad to observe, ineffective protest.

'You are fond of horses?' he asked. At that moment I was ready to be fond of anything, though, truth to tell, I am no fonder of a horse than I am of a cow or a bullfinch.

'Very', said I, with astounding conviction. So he took me to the stables, and we went from stall to stall for a long hour, during which we inspected thirty or forty clean-limbed, fine-crested brutes bred for speed and stamina. He talked a good deal in an ejaculatory kind of way, but I did not listen: I was occupied in studying this very singular man whose horsey face, with its broad upper lip, its gaping nostrils, and keen, pouch-enveloped eyes, told nothing of the delicate, sensitive artist's brain that functioned ceaselessly within his heavy skull. But suddenly I was called to attention by discovering that I was the object of a lecture on the subject of the docking of horses' tails.

'It's criminal - cruelly criminal!' he said in his mild, detached way. 'Brainless people imagine that the appearance of a horse is improved by cutting its tail off. You might as reasonably 'prettify' a lion by depriving it of its mane. These cutting and pruning people ought to be kept, stark naked and handcuffed, for a couple of hours, near a heap of manure: they'd soon know what it is to be tortured by flies.' Though his words were violent, his manner did not suggest that his emotions had been stirred in the least. We returned to the house, where other guests had assembled.

That lunch remains in my mind as a prolonged exasperation. The room was full of ponderous, elderly footmen, who, horribly distant in manner, seemed to imagine that, whatever their duties in life might be, it was certainly not their business to wait upon us.

True, a wing, with slow deliberation, was placed in front of me at some period of the meal, and I distinctly saw a lady hungrily depriving a peach of its stone. But some unknown power prevented the dishes on the sideboard from reaching the table. Walter Winans, the least conspicuous person present, lost all his importance. He seemed submerged in introspection, and towards three o'clock we rose, having lunched off champagne and the delicious odour of curried prawns.''

Gerald later listed that Winans was "a writer of books, a sculptor, a painter, a breeder of horses, a passionate hater of cruelty, a famous marksman, a terrific worker, a man who had seen the world and known its people. A strange man: an eccentric man." (Incidentally an American, if that fact has any special significance).

Many people would see little or no humour in that peculiar narrative, but I, not being a victim, found it hilarious - almost Gilbertian in fact. I would just like to make it clear that I actually love all animals, in the sense that I feel great compassion for them, and certainly share Winans' loathing of cruelty. But, like Gerald I have never had the least interest in any sport that involves animals. I love for instance to see horses running free,

131

but not exploited to provide entertainment for humans. However I must admit I am no vegetarian. Perhaps I am inconsistent as I am far from convinced that the slaughters are really humane.

Chapter Twenty Six

GERALD IN THE SHADOWS

Now that I am approaching the end of this strange muddled saga, I am going to find great difficulty in trying to fill in a few yawning gaps. Already I feel sure I will not succeed. Part Three was intended to be devoted almost entirely to Gerald's novel 'Lover at Forty.' On second thoughts I realised that it would be quite beyond my powers, but however skilfully it might have been achieved by abler hands, it would still have been a major blunder. Rightly or wrongly I had allowed myself to insert two or three references to the main characters, plus a few slight hints at the shaping of events. I never planned to re-tell the wonderful tale in abbreviated form to add an extra chapter. Such mutilation would have been nothing short of disastrous. For instance, to omit any of the magical phrases that do so much to create the unique atmosphere, would have been like stealing away its heart. However, I would willingly have sacrificed a number of (for me) irritating repetitions of intimate and endearing labels scattered about so profusely - Motherkin and Blond Beast worked to death, when even just once would have been one too many. Also, much overdone are Avril's 'husky voice' and 'dark beauty' which 'flowered into a smile' on the first page. That would be quite enough for some readers, a great pity as that opening chapter introduces the two hating-loving women (with emphasis on the 'hate') setting the scene fatefully. It was necessary to stress the physical contrast between Mrs. Colefax and her daughter Avril, but it could have been done

subtly and skilfully, so that we wouldn't need to be reminded
nearly every time they appeared. Also, all that flushing and
blushing, by no means confined to the ladies! In my youth,
blushing was the curse of my life, but I wasn't aware of any
other girl being so afflicted. If I had, it would have been so
much easier to endure. As it was, I could never hide my
confusion, even when all that was involved was a casual
encounter with any young male whatsoever. Other people
never turned red except in anger, or when being suddenly
'found out.' But those educated Edwardians - were the young
people (and not so young) all so sensitive? Now, at the end of
the hardened twentieth century, blushing teenagers must surely
be an extinct species!

Enough of that carping! Sorry Gerald, but I believe you
admitted to being a fellow-sufferer, at least until you handed on
the plague to me! For the rest of your novel - well-nigh
perfection!

One of Gerald's strong points was his rare ability never to let
his story flag; yet its pace is unhurried, with an undercurrent
almost sinister at times. Most of the characters throughout the
short span of time (only two or three months) give a superficial
impression of being just normal people enjoying mildly a
relaxed summer week-end. Yet half of them were anxious and
troubled in heart and mind in varying degrees. But Gerald
contrives a few masterly strokes of humour. Mrs. Colefax is
working out with consummate skill how best to capture her
prey, the rich Sir Rex who is to arrive later, but his plan deviates
from hers. When hers miscarries, her chagrin provides farcical
entertainment for the reader. She feels desperate, but must not
show it among the other guests. However Sir Rex is engineering
a simple campaign of time and place for his proposal, so all
should end well? After being suitably seduced by Mrs. Colefax's
singing, from a quiet corner of the room he informs her, "There
will be a moon this evening." No need for further comment!

This is my penultimate chapter, but Gerald's corresponding one from 'Written in Friendship' entitled 'Present Day Bohemianism,' I will pass over, except for one short paragraph of bitter nostalgia.

"Such is post-war intellectualism; such is the Bohemia of 1923. When I compare artistic and literary circles of to-day with those of 1913-14, I see that all that was good in Bohemia has vanished. Good-fellowship has gone, modesty is dead, and the only laughter that is left is like the crackling of thorns under a pot; our young hopefuls are eaten up with arrogance, smeared over with the ineffectiveness of crawling vanity."

That sums up the late hour of Gerald's prolonged pain. The knell is sounding.

Chapter Twenty Seven

FAITHFUL UNTO LIFE

My final chapter will be devoted mainly to 'The Survival of Man.' Can any of my readers suggest any subject of greater importance? Those of you with open minds (and who would like to admit having a closed one?) will I hope, bear with me patiently for the last time, while I struggle and grapple with the momentous question. As usual I have been unable to formulate a definite plan of development, but I am certainly not going to preach a sermon, or lapse into dogma. Personal experiences during this decade have convinced me that our souls do not die along with our bodies. Of course Christians profess likewise, but they diverge at the crucial point. I need not remind you of their claim that believers in their God are rewarded up aloft in Heaven while the non-believers (which of course includes many of 'us') find themselves (in polite football language) 'relegated' to the bottomless fiery pit called Hell, from which apparently no hope of escape is offered. Not many can really believe this still, but fear of punishment lurks uneasily for the thoughtful. Here I am tempted to wander unchecked on the subject of God, but at the moment I just wish to make it clear that my form of spiritualism is not a religion, although I have always been aware of the existence of the Soul.

I do not claim the ability to prove this, and will leave you all to think about the matter, discuss the pros and cons, and eventually come to some optimistic conclusion, or (more likely with the elderly) remain conservative. I propose, of course to include quotations from thinkers past and present. I will let the contributors speak for themselves, and any more comments I make will appear in the final paragraph.

I will begin with a very reputable seeker of truth whose statement is dated 1908 (the year of my birth), namely G. Lowes Dickinson, from 'Ingersoll Lecture on Immortality.' Harvard.

"It is mere dogmatism to assert that we do not survive death, and mere prejudice or inertia to assert that it is impossible to discover whether we do or not. We in the West have hardly even begun to inquire into the matter; and scientific method and critical faculty were never devoted to it, so far as I am aware, previous to the foundation, some quarter of a century ago, of the Society for Psychical Research.

Alleged facts suggesting prima facie the survival of death... are now at last being systematically and deliberately explored by men and women of intelligence and good faith bent on ascertaining the truth... I am asking you to take seriously a brand of scientific inquiry which may have results more important than any other that is being pursued in our time."

My second quotation is taken from the Summary of Sir Oliver Lodge's 'The Survival of Man.' At the time of my first birthday (November 1909) the book was first published, and ran into its fifth edition just two years later. That gives a good indication of the tremendous interest it aroused.

"Man's practical outlook upon the universe is entering upon a new phase. Simultaneously with the beginning of a revolutionary increase in his powers of physical locomotion - which will soon be extended into a third dimension, and no longer limited to a solid or liquid surface - his power of reciprocal mental intercourse also is in process of being enlarged; for there are signs that it will some day be no longer limited to contemporary denizens of earth, but will permit a utilisation of knowledge and powers superior to his own - even to the extent of ultimately attaining trustworthy information concerning other conditions of existence."

Lodge's 'Tentative Conclusion' follows, from which I cannot resist a few references.

"The evidence for the survival of man, that is for the persistence of human intelligence and individual personality beyond death, has always been cumulative; and now, through recent developments of the ancient phenomenon of automatic writing, it is beginning to be crucial.

The boundary between the two states - the known and the unknown - is still substantial, but it is wearing thin in places; and like excavators engaged in boring a tunnel from opposite ends, amid the roar of water and other noises, we are beginning to hear now and again the strokes of the pick axes of our comrades on the other side. So we presently come back out of our tunnel into the light of day, and relate our experience to a busy and incredulous, or in some cases too easily credulous, world. We expect to be received with incredulity; though doubtless we shall be told in some quarters that it is all stale news, that there has been access to the other side of the mountain range from time immemorial, and that our laboriously constructed tunnel was quite unnecessary.

Agile climbers may have been to the top and peeped over. Flying messages from the other side may have arrived; pioneers must have surveyed the route.

But we, like the navvies, are unprovided with wings, we dig and work on the common earth, our business is to pierce the mountain at some moderate elevation, and construct a permanent road or railway for the service of humanity. What we have to

139

announce, then, is no striking novelty, no new method of communication, but only the reception, by old but developing methods, of carefully constructed evidence of identity... The constructive ingenuity exists quite as much on the other side of the partition as on our side: there has been distinct co-operation between those on the material and those on the immaterial side. Let us not jump to the conclusion that the idea of 'space' no longer means anything to persons removed from the planet. They are no longer in touch with 'matter' truly, and therefore can no longer appeal to our organs of sense, as they did when they had bodies for that express purpose; but, for all we know, they may exist in the ether and be as aware of space as we are. Let us not be too sure that their condition and surroundings are utterly different from those of mankind. That is one of the things we may gradually find out not to be true. Meanwhile is there anything that tentatively we can say is earnestly taught to those who are willing to make the hypothesis that the communications are genuine?

The first thing we learn is continuity. There is no such sudden break in the conditions of existence as may have been anticipated; and no break at all in the continuous and conscious identity of genuine character and personality. Essential belongings, such as memory, culture, education, habits, character, and affection all these - for better for worse, are retained. Terrestrial accretions, such as worldly possessions, bodily pain and disabilities, these for the most part naturally drop away. Meanwhile it would appear that knowledge is not suddenly advanced - it would be unnatural if it were - we are not suddenly flooded with new information, nor do we at all change our identity; but powers and faculties are enlarged, and the scope of our outlook on the universe may be widened and deepened, if effort here has rendered the acquisition of such extra insight legitimate and possible. On the other hand, there are doubtless some whom the removal of temporary accretion and accidents of existence will leave in a feeble and impoverished condition; for the things are gone in which they trusted, and they are left poor indeed. Such doctrines have been taught, on the strength of vision and revelation - quite short of any recognised Divine revelation - for more than a century. The visions of Swedenborg, are not wholly unreal, and are by no means wholly untrue. There is a general consistency in the doctrines that have thus been taught through various sensitives, and I add my testimony to the rational character of the general survey of the universe made by Myers in his great and eloquent work."

I regret a little my inability to 'cut' but I find Lodge irresistible as he draws towards his conclusion. His book began with a detailed account of the origin of the Society for Psychical Research, and he has spared no pains to express clearly his deeply researched knowledge for the benefit of humanity.

I am fully conscious that it is now high time to make a giant leap from one end of the twentieth century to the other. Much of importance will be passed over during the process, but who knows? - I may fill in a few gaps later. At the moment I am itching to quote some remarkable contemporary female mediums and healers.

I am sure that Betty Shine will not mind that in my eulogy of her wonderful diverse gifts, I quote a little from the actual text of her 'Mind to Mind.' Her grandmother was a Spiritualist, and she herself (though unaware) a natural psychic from childhood. Later she discovered that she had developed tremendous healing powers. Her gift of telepathy extended to animals, for whom she had always felt a special love. She suffered greatly with her health for many years, before relief came when a well-known medium diagnosed her complaint as being caused by a build-up of unused energy. That meant a complete transformation of her life, which now became fully occupied with healing others.

This included absent-healing, in which for many years I felt I had little faith. At this point I would like to urge all my readers to accept its validity, as I have been compelled to do, after benefiting countless times from the uncanny skill of a young healer friend, Andrea. I will pass on Betty's message of assurance, which suggests that in many cases of pain, it is frequently possible for us to help ourselves, rather than rely on prayer, or at least, prayer alone.

"Each of us has been given mind energy to use. We should allow it to strengthen and expand, not keep it imprisoned within the confinement of limited beliefs."

Betty's life is so full and satisfying that one could continue indefinitely commenting on her endless experiences as a medium, healer and life-giver, but my necessary conclusion will be about death, which concerns all of us.

"Dying can be a joyful and even exciting appearance, and there is really nothing to fear. When we die, we are taken care of; there have been many accounts by people who have had near-death experiences, describing how they travelled down a tunnel, at the end of which they came to a bright light, and were greeted by someone who loved them.
Death is a birth into a new kind of life, and into further spiritual progress. Heaven and hell are within us both here and after death, and it is up to us to decide which we prefer. You cannot progress spiritually until you have let go and rejected materialistic values."

Much more recently I have made the acquaintance of another outstanding healer and medium, again solely through her writings. I refer to Doris Collins whose book 'Positive Forces' has done much to expand my mind still further.

"A positive mind can triumph over many ills," she affirms, which sounds like an echo of Betty Shine. Both of them possess great powers of mediumship and healing, but of course there are considerable differences to match their contrasting personalities. I will not stress these distinctions, but will rely mainly on quotes to cast additional light on to Doris's active experiences.

"When I communicate with the spirit world, part of me somehow leaves this plane - not normally the case with healing - and goes out into the alpha, the sphere of existence. The spirit world is not up in the clouds or down below the earth. It is all around us, and we are part of it. The psychic gift is like a delicate plant that needs watering. Nurture it correctly, and it will grow. Ignore it, and it will die."

That is what I personally always believed about what I called the 'Soul.' Doris continues:

"What is the use of developing a rare gift unless you can put it to good use? Although knowledge in itself is important, how one uses it is what really matters. We have gained great knowledge through science, but it is how we use science that is paramount. Atomic energy, for example, may save the world or destroy it. Used for the benefit of mankind, science is a wonderful thing; but it is also a monster that, wrongly used, can destroy us. Many of the apparent benefits of science have nasty side effects, and intelligent people rightly wonder about what we have done in the name of progress, and question things that we have so far taken for granted."

Doris goes on to discuss religions, and how many of them incorporate a belief in the after life, with the possibility of contacting those on the other side. She had stayed with North

American Indians, and learned at first hand what very psychic people they are.

"They firmly believe that their ancestors are crucial to their lives on this earth. Perhaps that is one reason why there seem to be so many Red Indian guides in the spirit world."

In her chapter 'How Psychics Function,' she avers that we still have much to learn, but sums up in such a clear direct way the answers we already know, that I hope she will forgive me for a rather long quote.

"We are on this earth for the purpose to progress and improve - to achieve and become greater than now. Let us strive to follow the path towards that fulfilment, remembering that we are surrounded by a great force of energy of which we are part. We must study, create and pass on our knowledge and experience for the benefit of others... The wonder and beauty of energy is that it is infinite. The secret of progress is to use this energy force around us, and think positively, if we are to cross the bridge to better times."

I have just decided that my last promised paragraph will chafe at such a restriction. I believe the spirits have ordained that it must have the status of 'Epilogue.'

EPILOGUE

As a link with the last chapter I would just like to add a note to Oliver Lodge's eloquent if naive vision of a tunnel-boring contact with the other side. He did well to admit that the constructive ingenuity exists as much on the immaterial side of the partition. In fact my own experience compels me to favour the view that F.W.H. Myers expressed as follows:

"It is not we who are in reality the discoverers here. The experiments which are being made are not the work of earthly skill. All that we can contribute to the new result is an attitude of patience, attention, care; and honest readiness to receive and weigh whatever may be given into our keeping by intelligences beyond our own. Experiments there are, probably of a complexity and difficulty which surpass our imagination; but they are made from the other side of the gulf, by the efforts of spirits who discern pathways and the possibilities which for us are impenetrably dark."

When I began my book, all I knew at the time was that Gerald had been my father, and it was wonderful to realise the tremendous affinity between us, as evidenced in his writings. But any idea that he might have survived in the spirit world had never entered my head. As far as I was concerned, no direct contact was ever dreamed of; therefore I entertained no idea of making any further move. I considered myself extremely lucky to have the three books which I would always treasure, to keep us close. In fact, like all my friends and relatives, we had

145

ignored the subject of possible death survival. I think that most people associated spirits with ghosts and skeletons, which we loved to be scared of as children, yet not even half believing. However, I personally revelled in Edgar A. Poe's 'Tales of Mystery and Imagination' long after adolescence.

I was therefore totally unprepared for all the manifestations following in the wake of my early chapters in which nothing could be construed as an overture to further connection.

I have now, I hope, let light into my innocent motives, with no idea of future developments here. I need not report again what must now be quite obvious to you all, namely that all the various dreams and sightings originated over the border by Gerald himself. What I wish to emphasise is my enjoyment of it all.

Never for a moment did I feel the slightest tremor of fear as to what might happen next. Gerald loved me as a brother I should say, and would never cause me any harm (even if occasionally deserved!) We learned very quickly to understand each other. I shared his ever youthful spirit of fun. I admit I was taken aback at the disappearance of the seat in the gardens, but I felt an affection for the poor little insignificant ghost dominated by his aged daughter!

I am learning all the time still, and realise I need not change drastically in order to be allowed a glad welcome beyond, with opportunities to learn, develop, and above all, help those in need whenever I am able, always with very special interest in and concern for children, cut off so young from earthly life.

I hope that in the first part of my Epilogue, I have cleared a few points regarding my own personal attitudes, beliefs and interests. As a diversion I would now like to stress the primary importance of language, and how in this century it has suffered considerably from abuse. First I will pick on the word 'class,' which I aim to eliminate completely from my vocabulary. This will raise many eyebrows among my Socialist friends, but I hope to convince at least a few of them of the harm it has done so far. I speak to the people of Britain in general, but to the English in particular. There is much talk of the Upper, Middle and Lower Classes. What does it amount to? Well, the words upper and lower conjure up a vertical ladder - with top, bottom, and various in-between rungs. I need not dwell on the Uppers, to whom of course we all look up with deference and admiration, not to mention envy, because they are rich! Those not born into that rarified atmosphere will have little chance to overcome all the obstacles blocking their advance.

Even the Upper Middles will be as likely to fall back as to rise. The Mid-Middles and Lower Middles are on the whole the most ambitious and determined to rise, hopefully with a 'good' education to help. Those poor wretches born and bred on the lowest rungs will mostly remain there, except for an odd few with innate ability, personality, quirky humour or supreme self-confidence, who make the grade, chiefly in the entertainment world.

There is even a faint possibility of rising to a dizzy pinnacle where anything might happen, including a Humpty Dumpty disaster. Now you all know these facts as well as I do. Let us end the whole rotten snob system, which has inevitably riddled our whole population with class consciousness and all its accompanying evils. The Upper Classes vote Tory almost to a Man (and Woman). They are a minority in number, but mighty powerful.

All above the Mid-Mids ape their 'betters', and only the lowest are so poor and without hope that they rarely bother to vote. Well then, where are the supporters of Labour? Where indeed, we may well ask? Where were they at the last four General Elections?

Thatcher had the brilliant idea of making it possible for vast numbers of people to own their homes for the first time. Out of gratitude they naturally supported her distinguished party.

147

Now, for heaven's (or rather earth's) sake, let us kick away that vicious ladder, and begin to think horizontally, so that we are freer to move forward toward the same goal, though at our own individual pace. What is the goal? No less than a simple, open life worth living. For the slow starters, they are more likely to find help on the way and greater fellowship, without the strain of climbing or just hanging on, never free from the danger of collapse. I speak specially to those who call themselves the Working Class. Why not simply 'the Workers', a name to rejoice in, immediately establishing yourselves as infinitely more important than the parasites at the top? I will end with a remark I heard from a woman acquaintance a few years ago, which has galled me ever since.

"I know a family with two cars, and they are only working class."

Note particularly the word 'only' (mere nobodies in fact). Come on all of you, men and women alike - overthrow this horrible counter productive class consciousness, along with racism. Let us respect each other for what we are worth to each other, and our usefulness to society in general. Don't let's be impressed by people for their wealth and possessions, but for their humanity, friendliness and sympathy for just causes. There are countless numbers of such people, especially among women and the young. Make your natural benevolence of greater real value by becoming political. It can also be fun to be on the left.

As for you men, revere Karl Marx, but not always his vocabulary! And let us lefties every one, struggle, Mandela-like to the end, hating all oppressors in the world, and loving their victims, using Pete Seeger's hammer of freedom, bell of justice and song of love as our weapons.

After re-reading my rambling anti-class tirade, I was reminded of John Major's claim to be working to produce a classless society: in fact he tries to give the impression that it had already been created the moment he became Prime Minister, for was he not one of us by birth? Actually he is very proud of his ability to rise to the commanding heights, although he must be uncomfortably aware of dangerous pitfalls ahead. Surely the British public, deliberately misled for so long, can at last see the light and realise the folly of being too trusting and gullible. Recently the lies and deceptions have surfaced alarmingly for the perpetrators. Now is our great chance to begin the overthrow in earnest. Let us enjoy the process, which can succeed if all the Broad Left unite, ignoring minor differences in the major cause. Of course the differences in our society are not all minor ones. In fact all individuals differ, which should add spice and interest to life. The clever ones must use their brains for the general benefit rather than to concentrate on self-interest. The main struggle must be towards full employment - there could be useful jobs to suit all who are able to work with brain or body, and no attitude of superiority or inferiority.

Let Marx be the link to my second choice of word, namely 'materialism' which he prefixed by 'dialectical.' This is no place for an explanation of his meaning, which is not within my power to attempt, even if I had the inclination. Like many other words now in common usage, it means different things to different people.

As a matter of curiosity I have consulted my ancient 'Concise Oxford Dictionary' which states: 'Materialism: Opinion that nothing exists but matter and its movements, also that consciousness and will are wholly due to material agency.' (Otherwise 'unspiritual.')

I have had numerous arguments with Marxist friends, especially about the existence or non-existence of the Soul. Having from quite early childhood, been aware that I was not merely a physical body, I had readily accepted the word Soul, partly I suppose in a religious sense, for several years, until I was old enough to understand the terms 'agnostic' and 'atheist.' The very idea of death being the ultimate end horrified me. I first encountered that atheistic view when no more than eight or nine years of age.

One of my few Saturday chores was to take a bucket to fill with coal from what we called the peat house. On one never-to-be-forgotten occasion, I discovered a pile of books in a dark corner. Being me, with an insatiable hunger for books, no matter how grimy and tatty, I picked one at random and made for the door and the only source of light for a good read. It was Robert Blatchford's 'God and My Neighbour.' It shocked me, as not to believe in God was unthinkable, in fact unendurable, therefore unacceptable. However a 'wicked' seed had nevertheless taken root in my mind (or Soul?) never to be eradicated. When I first went to live at Beckside, my eighty year old grandad was still alive, although failing, and I distinctly recall him in his rocking chair, where I enjoyed being gently rocked on his knee, while singing to the rhythm. I knew him for less than a year before he died, but never forgot him. I was informed later about his strong radical beliefs, combined with an increasing stand against the Conservative Church of England. None of this was lost on me. Also he was much opposed to alcohol, as certain families in the village were much impoverished in consequence of addiction by parents. If any tramps came round our way, they were never turned away empty, and were welcome to sleep in the dry barn, but were never given money for obvious reasons. So it was not surprising that reports of grandad's character and views played a definite part in my mental growth.

If I became an extremist, small wonder with at least one rebel on each side of my family. Grandad would no doubt qualify as a materialist from force of circumstances. Incidentally, he was a maker of coracle-shaped baskets.

We had few luxuries, but never went short of good plain food and warm clothing for the Winter; however the thrifty and abstemious habits of my grandparents meant that their youngest child (the aunt I lived with) who showed some musical ability, was allowed to have piano lessons. She later taught me to play, on the dear old fashioned instrument with its fretwork carving backed with green silk. So I realise that grandad was as well balanced as it was possible to be. Also he had a great thirst for book knowledge. His progressive mind welcomed all the late nineteenth century inventions, but when he heard that soon there would be flying machines on the way he flatly refused to believe beyond the easily understandable law of gravity. However by the time of his death in 1912 he had been proved wrong, though no doubt baffled to the end.

I realise that after his death my aunt would remove the more 'incriminating' volumes from our large bookcase, and shamefully relegate them to the 'black hole' at the back of the peat house. She had inherited no trace of her father's rebellious nature, and always aimed to appear ladylike and refined! She certainly never understood the way my mind worked. But I owe much to her warm loving devotion, though leaving me unprepared for life and its battles.

Gerald of course was almost devoid of materialism, and never approved of the 1917 Russian Revolution until he entered the spirit world of further education leading to the escalator dream, where we finally converged in mutual political understanding. My thoughts and concerns are always with the poor and downtrodden, who desperately need food, warm clothing, adequate shelter and medical aid, which after all come under the 'material' heading. However, let us remember that material acquisitions and possessions can find no place in the Spirit World, except as a bitter memory to some to haunt them until they discover how to exorcise the burden, as the Ancient Mariner finally rid himself of the dead albatross. The

151

concentration on Self has sooner or later to give way to a deep caring for all other beings, not just human ones, whether still in the Earth Life or sharing their Spirit World.

That is the message that comes across to me. But there will always be new lessons to learn and that means right now on our long-suffering Planet. Watch these men in Parliament and don't let them get away with selling arms to dictators, but make World Peace our Priority.

Finally, and briefly, I come to my third word, recently resurrected from obscurity by Mr. Kinnock, to help him invent a new kind of Socialism - Ethical, no less, which my dictionary assures me, means 'relating to morals.'

Now after a long period during which he eschewed the word Socialism altogether, perhaps he believes that a simple message has recently floated to him through the Ether where it originated before touring the galaxies to communicate with all beings attuned to receive it. Expect him now to use all his burning zeal to spread his new-found faith, but where is he likely to find disciples?

It won't be by getting Back to Basics either Neil.

Why not give simple Socialism the genuine trial it is waiting for? After all there already exists an Ethical Society, with sound humanitarian ideals. But ideological politics he has openly rejected. I have no faith in television solving our moral problems, nor yet any of the main religions, which so often breed wars.

Back to Basics - No! Let our movements all be Forward.

Learn from the Past - Yes.

Live for the Present - Yes.

Look to the Future - Yes.

With emphasis on improving prospects and happiness for children everywhere, as a result of the rejection of greed and selfishness, so rife among the prosperous capitalists.

It will be easier for them now than later, when the Workers and

Unemployed realise their true Destiny and United Strength, to face it with unfaltering Faith and Courage.

Finally, a few lines from Tennyson's stirring poem

'ULYSSES'

'Old age hath yet his honour and his toil.
Though much is taken, much abides; and though
Made weak by time and fate, yet strong in will,
To strive, to seek, to find, and not to yield.'